HELP!
I'M A GRANNY

HELP!
I'M A GRANNY

FLIC EVERETT

Michael O'Mara Books Limited

First published in Great Britain in 2015 by
Michael O'Mara Books Limited
9 Lion Yard
Tremadoc Road
London SW4 7NQ

A CIP catalogue record for this book is available from the British
Library.

Papers used by Michael O'Mara Books Limited are natural, recyclable
products made from wood grown in sustainable forests. The
manufacturing processes conform to the environmental regulations of
the country of origin.

Disclaimer: The information contained in this book is correct to the
best of the author and publisher's knowledge. Both the author and
publisher disclaim any responsibility from any medical consequences
that may occur.

ISBN: 978-1-78243-340-8 in hardback print format
ISBN: 978-1-78243-341-5 in e-book format

1 2 3 4 5 6 7 8 9 10

Jacket design by Billy Waqar
Illustrations from www.shutterstock.com
Designed and typeset by K DESIGN, Winscombe, Somerset

Printed and bound by CPI Group (UK) Ltd, Croydon, CR0 4YY

www.mombooks.com

Contents

Introduction

❝ Everyone needs to have access both to grandparents and grandchildren in order to be a full human being. ❞

Margaret Mead (Anthropologist)

There is no such thing as a typical granny. Old-fashioned picture books might suggest that she's a comfortable old body in a flowery pinny, grey hair piled in a bun as she knits baby bonnets – but no grandma has looked like that since 1923. In fact, nowadays, she's more likely to have highlights and be carrying an ensemble from Baby Gap in her Cath Kidston tote bag. Or she'll be working forty-hour weeks, trying to squeeze in some family time between Skype calls. Or she'll have planned to spend her retirement travelling round the Far East and learning to kitesurf, or be juggling 102 commitments, including elderly parents, a part-time job and a mid-life marriage.

Because grans are not what they used to be. The idea of a dear old woman drifting serenely into her twilight years, smiling benignly as the babies play at her feet is, frankly, nonsense. More likely she's still in the prime of life, trying to decipher scrawled instructions about puréeing butternut squash and folding up a buggy one-handed, while her daughter runs gratefully into the distance shouting, 'Back at teatime!'

So this book is not about knitting, or gentle walks in the park (though you can do both if you like). It's for every woman with grown-up kids who have suddenly revealed that they're having a baby. Because while there's endless advice for new parents, mums-to-be and nervous dads, there's not quite so much for grans who aren't remotely ready to put themselves out to pasture yet. And even if they were, the sudden appearance of a baby – or two, or three – can make that retirement fantasy somewhat redundant.

Nobody's assuming, of course, that you'll be at the coalface, changing nappies daily, tweezing mashed carrot out of the toddler's hair, or trying to recall the lyrics to any song that might get them to sleep.

You may, in fact, be living thousands of miles away, waving through the iPhone screen at your grandchildren, who are covered in sunblock and sitting on the beach. You may be at least a few hundred miles away, still living your own, very busy life, and setting reminders to yourself to enquire about how the birthday party went. Or you could be much nearer than that, seeing your grandchildren regularly, with all your cupboard door handles on childproof catches and the cake-making equipment on permanent duty.

Whichever type of grandma you are, I hope there will be something in this book to entertain and reassure you. Everyone expects new mothers to be nervous – after all, they have to go through childbirth, then get used to a whole new person with more demands than J-Lo travelling in Economy. But the worries that new grans have can be entirely overlooked in the flurry of excitement a new baby brings.

So settle back – though preferably not in a rocking chair – and prepare to discover everything you'll ever need to know about being a granny.

CHAPTER 1

The Shock of 'Gran'

❝ I didn't feel ready to be a grandma – I was only 49 and I felt I'd been pushed into a new life stage against my will. ❞

Anne Beddowes, 53

There is a general assumption that every woman wants to be a grandma one day. All the clichés revolve around the lonely older woman, begging, 'When will you make me a granny?' and nagging, 'Isn't it time you two started trying?'

But the reality can be quite different. Women in their 40s and 50s today tend to have more demands on their time than ever before – it's no surprise they're often referred to as 'the sandwich generation', spinning plates between ageing parents of their own, demanding jobs, money, marriage and young adult children who can often cause more sleepless nights than little ones. Suddenly throwing a new grandchild into the mix can be a terrible shock – and while you want to be delighted, and say all the appropriate things, often the first grandmotherly reaction to the joyous news is open-mouthed shock.

I was speechless. My daughter Lizzie was only 26, and very career-oriented. I really didn't expect her to get pregnant – she'd only been with her boyfriend James for six months, and I assumed she was being careful. She rang me up one Sunday morning, when I was reading the papers – to be honest, I had a bit of a hangover as we'd been to an anniversary do the night before – and said, 'I've got something to tell you, don't go mad.' My heart sped up, assuming she was in trouble of some sort. I asked her if she'd rather meet face-to-face, but she said she had to tell me straight away – then she blurted, 'I'm pregnant!' I know I paused for too long – it was so unexpected. Then I said, 'Is it what you want?' and she was immediately cross. She said, 'Can't you just be thrilled? James's mum is!' We had a slightly awkward phone call, where I tried to express my delight, without mentioning the fact that they live in a one-bed flat, and have no spare cash – but after she put the phone down, I'm afraid I felt tearful. I was worried for Lizzie – but selfishly, I also was afraid of how this would impact on my life.

Hester Baines, 58

A less-than-positive reaction isn't unusual – for every shriek of delight, there's a sudden inability to form words. The Hollywood dream where the big happy family hugs and cries with joy and starts building cherrywood cribs in the back porch is rarely what happens when an unexpected pregnancy is announced.

And while some grans-to-be are genuinely thrilled, and have waited long years to feel useful and rock a small baby to sleep again, plenty are poleaxed, trying to work out exactly what's going to happen to their lives in future. Will they be expected to sacrifice their free time? Be an unpaid childminder? Will they feel pushed out by a daughter-in-law who doesn't like them, or a son who's just taken a job at the other end of the country? Some may be dealing with illness – their own or a spouse's – or elderly parents, or coming to terms with retirement. Some may have settled into a pleasant, post-retirement pattern, and be fearful of disrupting it. And some grandmas may have absolutely no idea how they're going to fit a whole new family member into their already packed lives.

If you have been fully updated on the attempts to get pregnant (not in graphic detail, ideally) or have known for ages that your child and their partner are trying for a baby, then it may not be a shock at all – or at least only a joyfully positive one. In which case, excellent, crack open the cava (because you're drinking for two now your daughter can't) and log onto a baby-related website.

If you're somewhat surprised, however, you may well find yourself saying entirely the wrong thing. So here's a handy reference guide.

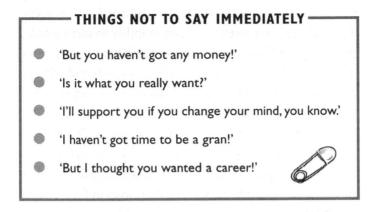

THINGS NOT TO SAY IMMEDIATELY

- 'But you haven't got any money!'
- 'Is it what you really want?'
- 'I'll support you if you change your mind, you know.'
- 'I haven't got time to be a gran!'
- 'But I thought you wanted a career!'

All of these can be said – more subtly – later on, if necessary, but the only possible thing to say when the pregnancy is announced – assuming your daughter or daughter-in-law is not sobbing piteously as she breaks the news – is, 'Wow! Congratulations, that's wonderful!'

The parents-to-be may well have their own fears and reservations – they don't need you listing pitfalls with a flip chart and a pointer. So now is not the time to bombard them with questions about how they're going to afford it, what they'll do about work, or what kind of childcare they'll be using. Those questions may arise spontaneously later or it may, in fact, be none of your business. Either way, the correct facial arrangement is 'wide smile' and the correct tone is 'overjoyed'.

This is perhaps the biggest shock for a gran-to-be because however much you long to meet the grandchild, their arrival suddenly kicks you right into a new life stage, with an unceremonious boot up the bum.

I was taken aback, when my son told me he was going to be a dad. In my mind, he's still a kid – even though he's 28, hairy, and living with his girlfriend. I suppose I assumed that he and Sarah would save up a bit, and get their fun out of the way with before they settled down. So when he told me that it was planned, I nearly said, 'But why now?' I managed to catch myself in time, and I hugged him instead, which gave me a minute to compose myself and be happy for him. Actually, I felt a bit left out that he didn't tell me they were trying for a baby. A bit of warning would have been nice, so I could deal with the idea of suddenly being a gran – it's such an odd concept when you're used to feeling quite youthful.

Alex Peters, 53

In the past, when women tended to have babies in their teens and 20s, maybe your late 40s was a time to let yourself go a bit, ease into middle age with a deflated sigh, and await grandmotherhood. But now, we're just getting going in our 40s. Work is busy, social lives are still boiling away – and though some of us are happily married, plenty of women are starting afresh in new relationships after a midlife divorce. Women with grown children no longer droop about at home, making scrapbooks of the vanished past and hoping for a visit – they're more likely to be at the gym, or raising money for charity, or out with mates at a wine bar, or on an internet date with some bloke who claimed to be a vibrant 52 and apparently knocked twenty years off his true vintage.

And there's not so much of the 'letting yourself go' either. Chance would be a fine thing! Most women over 45 have got bathroom cabinets stuffed with everything from extract of horse urine, to herbal Botox, to hair-and-nail pills, all to help them stay feeling and looking youthful and attractive. Half of them have taken up running, and are constantly posting pictures on Facebook of themselves in designer leggings and hi-tech trainers, grinning at the top of some craggy mountain peak. And the other half are too busy at work, or starting a new online business in the spare room, or planning their next exotic holiday to go running, so instead they're having facials and getting their nails done like some high-powered New York chairwoman of the board. These women do not have 'Gran' hovering over their heads, any more than their busy 50-something husbands have 'Grandad'. Because ageing men don't look like the old guy in *Up* any more, either.

This baby-boomer generation grew up in the fifties, sixties and seventies. They smoked when they shouldn't, and danced to music their parents didn't understand. They probably took drugs of some kind at some terrible nightclub, and then realized their friend had got in a stranger's Ford Cortina and gone home without them. They were the first to have regular package holidays, the women who stormed the workplace, packed the kids off to childcare, and recognized that divorce wasn't a badge of shame. These are not cosy, naïve old people we're talking about here, but women in the full flow of life, who have suddenly realized that time has marched on and they're no longer just a busy mother, they're a grandma, with all that entails.

Most of us base our certainties about grandmotherhood on what our own grans were like or our own mums. So if we don't instantly feel we match up, it's probably because we have a certain blueprint in our minds.

Here are some of the things you might think being a grandma means:

✳   Always being available for childcare

✳   Getting old

✳   Feeling and looking old

✳   Being the oldest generation of the family

✳   Being eternally patient

✳   Not working

✳   Cooking, gardening, sewing – all the domestic skills that a proper old lady has tucked under her apron

✳   Wearing an apron

✳   Not swearing

✳   Not shouting

✳   Not understanding modern music

Actually, that last one may be a given past the age of 40. But as for the rest, they're some ridiculous cliché of grandmotherhood, and it's unlikely you feel anything like that (imaginary) person. Maybe your own grandma had a perm like steel wool, and a crocheted cardi with pockets full of lavender-scented tissues and cough drops (actually, your grandma might have flown round the world in a biplane and called all her lovers 'Toots' for all you know) – but it doesn't mean you have to do the same. When your child has a child, you're still a grandma, whether you're running a Nevada brothel, signing off vast sums of corporate money while wearing haute couture, or just sitting about in a tiger-print onesie watching trashy daytime television because there's nothing else on. Because the word 'grandma' describes a familial relationship, not the sort of person you're expected to be.

It's true that emotionally, while being a gran-to-be can be uplifting, joyous and welcome, it can also mean a shift in the way you view yourself. Few of us now want to be seen as 'the older generation' – even if we are. And being 'a granny' suggests a certain set of attitudes and behaviours, which can have an impact on your self-image and confidence.

The reality of grandmotherhood is often very different from the fantasy but initial fears about what it means to be a gran, how much contact you'll have with the baby, whether there will be arguments or even if you should give up work (as many grans do to provide affordable childcare) can all seem overwhelming. A straw poll of fifteen grandmas aged 45 to 72 suggested that news of the pregnancy immediately kicked off the following various worries:

* How will my child cope? She can barely do the washing-up, let alone have a baby

* I haven't got time to be a granny

I found that thinking of myself as a granny was a shock at first. I feel quite vibrant and I've got kids who are still in their 20s, so even though my eldest daughter is 32, it didn't strike me that I'd have a grandchild so soon. I was thrilled, but also, deep down, a bit scared of what it would mean for my freedom. My daughter Elise hinted right away that she hoped I'd be a big part of the baby's life, just as my mum was in Elise's, and while I hoped to see lots of her, I was also aware that I might be expected to make a lot of sacrifices if Elise went back to work and asked me to mind the baby.

Another thing that bothered me was how the world sees grandmas – there's a sort of perception that they're old, taking a back seat and that all you'll have to talk about is your grandkids. I cringe at that perception, because I'm not like that, so it took a bit of adjusting.

Lynne Keller, 60

* Will I be expected to give up work to look after it?

* What if they move away and I never see the grand-child?

* I'm not ready to be a grandma – I'm not even meno-pausal yet!

* I feel so old

* I've forgotten everything I ever knew about child care – what if I harm the baby?

* Will I be a poor second to the maternal grandparents who live nearer?

* They haven't got enough money – we'll have to sup-port them

But after the first year, their original worries were almost all completely irrelevant.

Here's what really happened . . .

* The (28-year-old) child coped fine, and is now back at work while grandma looks after the baby two days a week

* She found the time – every other weekend for a visit suits both parties

* No, she wasn't expected to give up work – the mum decided to use the crèche at her office

✳   They haven't moved away and have no plans to do so

✳   There's no such thing as 'ready' and she's delighted with her grandson

✳   She isn't old

✳   She remembered quite quickly, with the help of a couple of websites

✳   No, there seems to be room for everyone, despite the occasional stab of jealousy

✳   They gave a gift of £1,000 and since then the parents are managing

Of course, worries can come true but it's worth remembering that women have always had babies, and older women have always become grandmas as a result. And usually, it turns out just fine.

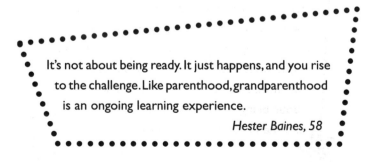

It's not about being ready. It just happens, and you rise to the challenge. Like parenthood, grandparenthood is an ongoing learning experience.

Hester Baines, 58

I'd been with my partner for a couple of years – after a rocky divorce in my 40s, things were just settling down, I was happy at work, and felt I had a new lease of life. I was excited when my son told me he and his wife were having twins, but I also felt suddenly less attractive. It even had an impact on my sex life. I kept thinking, 'I'm a granny now, I shouldn't be doing this!'

I knew it was nothing to do with how I felt about myself really, but whenever I told people I was going to have a grandchild, I was aware that I was bracketing myself with older people for good – that any illusion I had of still being young were gone. It didn't help that I'd just gone through the menopause, too, which I found difficult physically and emotionally – so it was as if I'd aged overnight. My partner was very understanding, even though I felt selfish and silly admitting my issues around grandmotherhood, and a few of my friends had also recently become grannies, so we could talk about what that felt like. My granddaughter is two now, and I can't believe I was so worried about being a gran. I'm just 'Nanny Sue' now, and she's brought me so much joy.

Susan Morton, 55

CHAPTER 2

PREGNANCY, CHILDBIRTH AND WHAT YOU CAN DO ABOUT IT

❛ I'd forgotten everything about what it felt like to be expecting a baby – my daughter had to remind me how hard it can be. ❜

Leah Wilson, 50

No offence, but it's probably been a while since you had a baby. And while some women have a wonderful time with every minute of pregnancy, they are the exception rather than the rule, so it's no wonder that we tend to forget the bad bits once we get to the 'cute bundle in a blanket' part. Which means that when your daughter, or daughter-in-law, announces her pregnancy, remembering what that actually feels like might be a bit like trying to recall the questions you answered on your O Level geography paper. But you'll want to support her through it, any anxieties she's having, and understand what stage she's at, how big your future grandchild is – the size of a bean, ping-pong ball or giant Buddha statue – and when the nine months and two weeks of pregnancy (though it's almost never accurate) is up she may ask you to be there for the birth. And that's when you'll definitely want to know exactly what's going on.

It was 32 years since I'd had Anna and 35 since I had her brother Jamie. My pregnancy with Anna was really difficult – I was sick throughout, and I was worried about passing on my feelings about my own experience to my daughter. She wanted to know how it had been for me but I didn't want to tell her the truth as it was awful. I was really worried for her – I expected the worst and I think I passed that feeling on to her, as she was a nervous mum-to-be. As it turned out, she only suffered a bit of morning sickness, and her birth was totally straightforward. She's planning another baby, and this time, I'll be a lot more relaxed.

Terri Harper, 63

Every woman experiences pregnancy differently so it's helpful if you try not to let your own experiences affect your attitude. But no matter how easy – or not – her pregnancy, there are certain symptoms that are likely to strike her at some point. So here's what they'll look like, how they'll feel, and what you can do about them.

COMMON PREGNANCY SYMPTOMS

Morning sickness

This can strike from the first month, and usually eases off by the fourth month, or second trimester. It can take any form, from mild occasional nausea to violent vomiting, and 'morning' isn't always true – it can last all day.

SHE'LL FEEL: Miserable, bad-tempered and unwilling to go anywhere where sudden vomiting might be a problem (which is nearly everywhere).

DO: Offer sympathy, buy her ginger biscuits (which may alleviate the nausea) and offer to do her shopping/ look after her if her partner's not around to do it.

DON'T: Suggest she's exaggerating, expect her to eat what you've cooked, or be offended if she absents herself from gatherings for a while – constant nausea is hugely debilitating.

Fatigue

Pregnancy causes serious tiredness. Your party-girl daughter-in-law may start going to bed at 8 p.m., and feel the need to subside into an armchair regularly, particularly if she's still working.

SHE'LL FEEL: Knackered, for the first and last trimester particularly. The magical second trimester should offer a bit of respite, but by the time the baby's feet are on her bladder and its head is shoved up in her lungs, even the simplest task can be an effort.

DO: Recognize that she's genuinely exhausted, she's not just whinging for no reason. Offer occasionally to make dinner and drop it round if you're nearby, help with housework or run an errand for her. Practical support is ideal.

DON'T: Forget what it feels like to be worn out – don't be upset if she doesn't answer calls because she's gone to bed, or cancels meeting up for lunch.

Mood swings

Pregnancy plays havoc with hormones so she may be irritable, weepy or swing miserably between the two. Again, in the second trimester, this should improve as things settle down.

SHE'LL FEEL: Confused by her own ridiculous over-reactions, embarrassed, upset, but unable to stop herself feeling what she feels – no matter how silly it may seem to everyone else.

DO: Exercise patience. She's not doing it on purpose, so when you offer a cup of tea and she snaps, 'You know I don't drink tea any more!', remind yourself that it's not her, it's the hormones – mainly to avoid pouring it over her head.

DON'T: Snap back, say, 'There's no need to be so moody, madam!' or attempt to get her partner on your side by saying, 'Is she like this with you?' A little ignoring goes a long way.

Taste changes

Pregnancy often makes familiar food taste revolting – so it's entirely possible that she'll go off tea, coffee and any combination of foods that suddenly taste metallic and unpleasant to her. A few months in, she might develop cravings for a particular taste.

> **SHE'LL FEEL:** Revolted by the things she used to like, a little freaked out that she can't stand her favourite foods any more, and awkward that she has to warn everybody to make her separate food if she visits.

> **DO:** Adapt to her needs – make a list of what she can eat and drink, and try and keep some of her favourite things in for when she visits.

> **DON'T:** Overlook her tastes – if she really can't stand the taste of fish, and you cook fish pie on the basis that she'll get over it, it's no one's fault but yours when she's starving.

Other symptoms may include: swollen feet and ankles, breast pain, insomnia, backache, headaches, faintness, anaemia, anxiety.

WHEN TO WORRY

All of the above symptoms are a pain for her to live with, but not life-threatening. However, there are a few conditions that can be very dangerous, so if she seems to be exhibiting the following, suggest she sees a doctor ASAP.

❋ Bleeding – spotting can be normal but should be checked by a doctor or midwife. More intense bleeding, with cramps, could be a sign of an ectopic pregnancy or a miscarriage. She needs to go to hospital.

❋ Severe morning sickness – if she really can't keep anything down, she could get severely dehydrated, a danger for both her and the baby.

❋ The baby stops moving. Some babies are very serene but if it's normally active but then there's no movement over a few hours, call the doctor to be on the safe side.

❋ Severe headache, visual disturbance, stomach pain or swollen legs in the third trimester – these could be a sign of pre-eclampsia, which causes high blood pressure and is extremely dangerous, so she must go to hospital.

My son is away a lot for work, so I see my daughter-in-law every few days. When she was seven months pregnant, I noticed she had badly swollen ankles. She said she'd been walking around too much, but they didn't look normal to me – she's very slim and they were really ballooning up. I suggested she should call the doctor, but she brushed it off saying she'd be fine. I had a real dilemma whether or not to interfere. After a couple of hours' agonizing, I decided I'd rather be interfering than risk something terrible happening, so I rang the doctor and they told me to take her to hospital to be checked. She wasn't very happy, but it turned out she had severe oedema and they needed to check for pre-eclampsia. Thankfully, she didn't have it but I was glad I'd made the call.

Jane Earnshaw, 49

The problem for grandmothers-to-be is, when should you interfere and when should you back off? As a general rule, the only possible excuse for interfering is when you truly believe that she or the baby are in danger. However, nagging about her diet: 'I'm sure I read that too much sugar is bad for the foetus', fretting that she's going out too much: 'Are you sure noisy bars are a good idea?' or expressing shock if she has half a glass of wine: 'Really? Are you sure? Foetal alcohol syndrome can be extremely dangerous', are all unacceptable. She is a grown woman, your son (or son-in-law) is a grown man. They are capable of making their own decisions, even if they're not ones you agree with. So the greatest thing you can do as a grandmother-to-be is to bite your lip and if necessary, place tape across your entire mouth, rather than blurt, 'How can you think that's a good idea?' The interfering mother/mother-in-law is a stock character in sitcom and you do not want to be known as 'the nag bag' behind your back, or to be the person who makes your family breathe a sigh of relief when you finally leave.

Which brings us to . . .

THE NAMING BIT

Pregnancy is the time when the prospective parents are going to be thinking about a name. And while some prefer to meet their child first, and decide if he looks like a Rufus, or she looks like a Matilda, most spend some time debating possible names prior to the birth. And unless you're from an ancient family whose boy children are invariably called after the male before, and whose middle names recognize the great-great-great-grandfather who was private secretary to Queen Victoria, you may well be expected to deal with some possibilities you're none too keen on. Your imagination will immediately fly to the day you're out in the park, pushing the pram, and a kindly stranger peers in and coos, 'Oh, lovely, what's its name?'

and you have to say 'Des'ree L'Amour' or 'Ziggy Zion Selassie' or 'Rooney Ferguson Scholes'.

You may also be aware that the classic name the parents think is wildly charming and original will be on every other pencil case come the start of Year One. Among the most popular baby names in Britain in 2014 were Ella, Scarlett, Eva, Amelia, Poppy, Ruby and Lily – basically, any collection of modern girl babies sounds like a *Downton Abbey* below-stairs casting call – while boys' names included old favourites Harry, Jack, Oliver, Thomas and George – turning boy babies into First World War characters.

So while you may be itching to comment – perhaps you'd like them to drop 'Summer Beyonce' in favour of Grace, or swap 'MoJo Max' for 'Archie' – or maybe you'd prefer a more unusual name, or for them to consider naming the baby after your mother, or your husband, or even yourself. But the rule is, you're permitted a couple of mentions, at the most. Feed your suggestion into the system, casually: 'I've always thought Sarah is a lovely name. Like your great-aunt . . .' then retire gracefully from the discussion, unless your opinion is directly canvassed. If it is, aim to avoid sounding snobbish, old-fashioned or obsessive ('I just don't see what's wrong with naming him after Grandad – Monty is a lovely name'). Otherwise, you're only allowed to comment if you realize that the baby's initials will spell out something terrible that will get him or her teased for ever, at which point, for God's sake, speak up and stop them calling him Frederick Archie Taylor before it's too late.

My daughter and her partner had a long list of possible names; some I liked and some I loathed. I made the mistake early on of suggesting they shouldn't pick something so unusual that the child would be teased, or spend his life spelling it out for people, and they were quite withering – 'Everyone has unusual names now,' and so forth. That's true, and their eventual choice was Rhiannon, which I wouldn't have picked myself, but I don't mind it. I am aware it's not up to me but it's odd because you know you're going to have a lifelong relationship with that child, and its name is important.

May Hillier, 63

As well as the baby's name, of course, there is the thorny issue of your own. Because what you decide to be called will stick for good and you'll be at that baby's wedding in thirty years' time, with people saying, 'Aah, look at Noo-Noo's dancing! Isn't she amazing for 87?' So if you don't want to be called Noo-Noo for ever, now's the time to say so. Of course, your grandchild may have her own opinions and if she wants to call you Gaggit, or NerNer, she will. It's up to you if you go along with it. But don't bother with all the 'I'm not old enough to be a granny' nonsense – nobody wants to see a three-year-old looking trustingly up at you and saying, 'Can I have a biscuit, Sheila?'

If your child is old enough to have kids, then you're old enough to be a granny. And you need a name. If your own mum is still around, she'll need one too. Then there's the in-laws, who will also be jockeying for gran position, and if you long to be called 'Nanna' and the other Grandma bags it first, you won't be happy. Ideally, you'll either be 'Nanna Jane' and 'Nanna Sheila', or you'll go with Granny, or whatever variant you choose, while she sticks with 'Nanny'. But a little early discussion over names saves an awful lot of disappointment later on.

I hadn't thought at all about what I'd be called. I suppose I just assumed I'd be called 'Grandma', as that's what my children always called my mum – my husband's mum was known as 'Nan'. But then when Tilly was born, my daughter-in-law's mum decided that she was going to be 'Grandma' and to be honest, I felt a bit pushed out. I suggested we could be 'Grandma Jane' and 'Grandma Elizabeth' but that was quite a lot for a toddler to say – Tilly ended up calling me 'Ganage' so that's what I'm now called. I expect I'm stuck with it, but it makes me laugh when she says it, so I don't mind. I wish I'd thought about it a bit earlier though.

Jane Earnshaw, 49

If you don't speak up early on about your expectations, the chances are you may end up stuck with more than a name you don't fancy. The most important issue for any prospective gran is involvement – what's expected, will you be offering childcare or simply be a social visitor, and how much time can you realistically offer – not to mention negotiating the fine line between help and interference.

And while some mums and dads leave all the arrangements until the baby's born because they don't want to tempt fate, or they're just a bit disorganized, or they don't know whether they're going to work full-time, part-time or not at all – if you can possibly agree certain basics, it can make life infinitely smoother once you're plunged into the chaos of a newborn. You don't want to be ringing your daughter shouting, 'I thought we should talk about childcare tax relief,' over the sound of a howling infant.

So sometime after the six-month point, when it's looking pretty certain things are OK, and she's had a chance to recover from nausea and exhaustion, and think about the future, suggest you have a chat about your involvement. It may seem strange and artificial to define boundaries and make agreements but if you're planning to be deeply involved in childcare, it's sensible to give yourself time to plan, particularly if you intend to give up work, or reduce your hours.

Some grandparents also decide to move closer when a baby's on the way but that entirely depends on the sort of relationship you have with your child. You don't want to announce, 'Guess what? We've bought the house next door!'

while popping a cork, only to be met with stony silence. If you like your own space too, then you may need to gently introduce the idea of what will be expected – are you going to have the baby for overnight stays, or will you go to them to babysit? What are their plans regarding childcare? And if you're in the Mary Poppins hot seat, will you charge or not? Some grandmas would faint at the very idea of taking a penny. Others see it as a service that requires expenses at the very least. And if you're giving up work to look after your grandchildren full-time, that's a very different story from taking them to the park once in a while.

Nobody wants to sit down with their mum and fill in a form ('How many hours will you expect to work in the first year? Will you be taking public transport to your workplace?') but it is useful to have the conversation before unspoken expectations creep in, swiftly followed by anger or disappointment. Even checking how much help they'd like at first is a thoughtful approach because while some new grans move in with the new parents, sleeves rolled up ready to sterilize midnight bottles like a crack SAS squad, others hang back, afraid of intruding and waiting (often fruitlessly) to be invited round.

Few new parents, however, can face inviting anyone round formally because the house will look as though a depth charge exploded in a charity shop, he'll be gaunt and hollow-eyed, and she'll be wearing the same dressing gown she put on last Thursday and hasn't yet removed, desperately leafing through parenting manuals and feeling sick with guilt, because the baby's crying and she doesn't know why.

So ask before it's born: 'Do you want privacy or would you prefer some help?' If you live far away, and you suspect that they want bonding time together without you, consider booking a hotel for a couple of days so you'll be on hand, but they don't have to worry about finding clean sheets for the spare room, or what you're going to eat for breakfast.

CHILDBIRTH

This is the sharp end. (And the painful, shrieking, how-will-I-ever-get-it-out end.) You'll probably be almost as nervous as the parents are about the birth itself, particularly if it's the first time. And three things can happen: You'll either be at home, biting your nails and clutching the phone, while your partner says, 'These things take time,' and slugs brandy. Or you'll know nothing about it until the giddy phone call at 8 a.m. where the new dad shouts, 'EIGHTPOUNDSTWOOUNCESITSAGIRL!' down the phone, and nobody can hear anything for joyous screaming. Or, scariest yet perhaps most exciting of all, you'll be asked to be there for the birth. If you don't think this is an option for you, these are the reasons to say no if you're asked:

✻ You faint at the sight of blood and will be more trouble than you're worth to everyone

✻ You're phobic about hospitals

There aren't any other reasons. If you're asked to be there, it's an honour, and your job is to show up, say soothing things, and cradle the new baby while everyone else cries and changes their sweat-drenched clothes. Pack a bag with a change of clothes (just in case there's a few bodily fluids knocking about), wet wipes (they're useful for everything in the world), snacks (because you might get sick of vending-machine crisps by the ninth packet) and a book, in case there's a very long wait in between things actually happening. (If you don't, you'll be stuck in the waiting room watching 24-hour news.)

Obviously, you can't book time off work as you don't know when it will be, but if your boss is reasonable give advance warning. If not, cross your fingers and hope the mother-to-be goes into labour on a Friday night.

That's all wonderful but if you're not asked, it doesn't mean that nobody cares about you. It's very likely, if you're the paternal grandma, that your daughter-in-law will want her own mum there, or her sister, or best friend. And even if it is your daughter, there's no rule that says women must have their mothers attend the birth, as this is not 1532, and there's no need to have women of the bedchamber hanging about to verify that the prince was truly born of royal blood. Often, too, the mother will want no one but her partner to see her in the state she's about to find herself in, or to share the first moments of their baby's life. Because usually nowadays, the father-to-be is not lurking outside the hospital, smoking nervously. He will probably, in fact, be on the other side of the bed, while she grips his hand in a death-clench and swears off sex for ever. And you may not want to be around for that.

If you aren't there for the birth – or you get stuck in traffic and miss the main show – it isn't a disaster. Being a grandma is not a competition so turn up as soon as you're permitted, praise the other grandma for her sterling work at the bedside if necessary, and then open your arms and say hello to the new baby. Whatever you do, don't curdle the atmosphere with regret or resentment, the main thing is the baby's safe arrival, not your place in the imagined 'best grandma' hierarchy. But it may take a while to sort out which grandma does what, and renegotiate new family relationships, now there's a baby involved – and babies are like Hollywood stars: everyone wants a piece of them. So let's look at how to avoid jealousy and find out what kind of grandma you're going to be, whether hands-on, full-on, or on Skype.

I was both honoured and terrified when Anna and her partner asked if I'd be there for the birth. They were worried he'd get stressed watching her in pain, and she liked the idea of me being there to welcome my grandchild. Also, if it took ages, it meant he and I could take it in turns to have a quick break. We had a few false alarms – she went to hospital once and it turned out to be Braxton-Hicks contractions. I was already in a taxi, so I had to tell the driver to turn round and take me home again. But three days later, it was the real thing. Her partner, Pete, rang me at 6 a.m., and I've never been out of bed so fast. Anna was fine till about 11 a.m., when the pain started in earnest – I held one hand and Pete held the other – there was a hairy moment when it looked like the cord might be wrapped round the baby's neck, but it was OK, she came out in a rush, and I was holding her within seconds. I was just overwhelmed with love. It was honestly one of the best moments of my life.

Terri Harper, 63

CHAPTER 3

GRANDMA VERSUS GRANDMA

❝ I didn't want to feel jealous but Pam was the maternal grandma, and she lived nearer. I found myself counting up the time I spent with my grandson, and comparing it to her almost-daily visits. It was hard not to feel pushed out. ❞

Ann Harrison, 65

'The jealous are troublesome to others, but a torment to themselves,' said writer William Penn, and just because you're older and allegedly wiser, it doesn't mean you're immune to feeling envy, or that you won't feel insecure about your place in the baby's life.

Those emotions can begin right from the start; it's often, though not always the case, that the daughter's mum tends to see more of the baby. If your son is the slightly more distant type, who seldom rings or lets you know what's going on (i.e. a man), it can feel as though you've been pushed out of the happy family circle.

Conversations that begin 'When Jane was here yesterday, she said . . .' or 'Laura's mum thinks . . .' may all sow seeds of uncertainty about your place in the baby's life. And it can be particularly difficult if you're living much further away, reduced to irregular visits and the odd Facetime session; or if you're still working, and the other granny is devoting herself to childcare.

Or maybe you feel you don't get on that well with your son or daughter-in-law and they're not that keen on your visits, or that the other grandma hears all the baby news first. It can be particularly tricky if you're a step-grandparent, too. It's hard not to feel as though the biological, 'real' grandparent is already ahead, that somehow, they love the grandchildren more than you

I live 200 miles away from my family. Susannah and her boyfriend, David, live in London, and when she got pregnant I secretly hoped they'd move back to Yorkshire but they're staying put. That means David's parents are just a couple of tube stops away. I see on Facebook that Susannah and Dave have been out, and inevitably, Claire and Jim would have babysat for them. They also have the grandkids to stay regularly. I know we can't afford to move and we don't really want to live in London, but I do feel very envious as we only get a couple of visits a year.

Wendy Shields, 59

do, because they're 'blood' and that their place in the family is assured, while you're seen as the grandad-snaring wicked step-mother, who must be tolerated but not fully embraced.

Modern families can be a stew of steps, halves, divorces, remarrieds and cohabiters, with lesbian and gay parents, single parents, much older parents, IVF multiple births or accidental parents thrown into the mix. It can be hard to know what your role is as a grandparent and where you fit in. You're no longer a hands-on mum, and you've probably got used to caring at a distance. But suddenly, you may be thrust right back into the heart of family life – or at least, hope that you will be. And nobody knows the rules.

Jealousy is an insidious emotion; you may determinedly tell yourself you're being silly, but it will creep in anyway. It's basically fear – that you're missing out, that you're not good enough, or that you won't have the relationship you want with your grandchildren. And it can all too easily turn into martyrdom.

And all of the above will harden the hearts of your dear ones towards you, and make them sigh, 'Oh God, Mum's kicking off again.' Because when a couple (or a singleton) has a new baby, they simply want all the help they can get, and like animals running from an earthquake, they'll take any shelter and support that's available. It's not because they think you're a lesser grandparent, it's expedience, pure and simple. And while it may hurt to know that other grandparents are spending hours cuddling and feeding, bear in mind that children tend to love grandparents equally, based on how kind they are not how often they see them.

The point is, it's easy to feel left out, but you never know what the future will hold – in a few years the landscape may look very different.

But if it's more than simple distance that's causing the problem, it's essential that you look at what's really happening. Here are the issues you might face and how to handle them . . .

THINGS YOU SHOULD NEVER SAY, NO MATTER HOW JEALOUS YOU FEEL

- Which grandma do you love best?

- I see she was babysitting again. I hope she didn't ply them with sweets like last time.

- When are you coming to stay here? Because you seem to be constantly at their house.

- How much did they spend on those presents? It's ridiculous.

- I suppose we can't compete.

- Well, it's clear who you prefer to spend time with these days.

When my first grandchild was born, my son and his wife lived in America. I could only afford a trip once a year, so we managed on Skype and Facebook, but I longed to spend more time with them. Ellen's parents are American and they'd go over regularly. They're lovely people, but it was hard not be jealous. But when Sonny was three, Alex's job was shifted back to the UK. It means I see Sonny every other week – it's a joy, but now I feel for Ellen's mum and dad. We're planning a big family reunion at ours next time they visit.

Sheila Kennedy, 67

1 You feel the other grandma is taking over

If she's always there when you go round, like some interfering fairy godmother, bending over the crib, knitting indeterminate pastel items, and generally carrying on like something out of *Sleeping Beauty*, you may feel like an interloper. This other grandma (let's call her the O.G.) has inserted herself entirely into the family's life and is full of detailed information: 'She sicked up 15 ml of carrot puree at 11.05, but the muslin squares are in the wash, aren't they, darling, and we've got a tooth coming through in the second canine position . . .' while you feel like some vague idiot who's just about grasped what gender the baby is. She's made herself indispensable and you're just a passing visitor.

What To Do

There is no reason to compete. How lovely for a baby to have two lots of adoring grandparents – and how much better if you both offer different things. When the kid's seven, she'll be driving him mad, spitting on hankies and scrubbing his face and enquiring after his nutrition levels. You, meanwhile, can be Cool Grandma, who is fun and chilled out and knows how to use an iPhone. Don't get sucked into competitive grandparenting – let her obsess, and enjoy your more relaxed time with the baby.

23 There are too many grandparents

There's her parents, his original parents, his dad's second wife, her dad's partner . . . It's hard to get a look-in, when they're virtually queuing round the block for a go of the new baby. Then there's their friends, aunties, uncles, brothers and sisters, all of whom want their moment in the newborn-cuddling sun. It can be frustrating, and envy-inducing when you hear that their weekend was spent entertaining the step-gran-in-law, and you're miles away, waiting for an invitation into the royal presence.

What To Do

Book in advance. It's no good waiting about for an invitation like a nervous Cinderella. Others won't be quite so diffident and they'll be the ones steaming in for a visit while you're at home thinking 'best not intrude'. So ring the parents, say, 'When suits you?' and if they can't commit: 'Well, Dan's parents are coming on Saturday, then Shelley and Steve are round on Sunday, then . . .' simply make a suggestion that doesn't entail huge effort on their part. Sometimes a walk in the park is a lot more doable than inviting yourself for lunch (because then they'll have to tidy and provide food and find fresh milk for tea etc.) or offer to have the baby for a couple of hours while they sleep. And if your time is limited, due to work, or distance, make sure you make a firm booking weeks ahead, and call a week beforehand to gently remind them. It can also be wise to befriend the other grandparents, so you can share news and pictures, if you haven't done so already.

3 You don't feel needed

They're so well organized with childcare, possibly provided by the O.G., you can't see a gap for you to fit into. The parents are working in the week, you don't want to interfere by turning up at the O.G.'s house, but at the same time, it seems there's just no room for you. Once, grandparents might have provided equipment for the baby, clothes, babysitting services, even cooking for the exhausted parents. But when that's all been taken care of already, and the parents want to spend their own family time with your grandchild at weekends, how do you find a role?

What To Do

Ask. Simple but effective. Saying 'I'd love to be more involved – what would work for you?' is a lot more likely to get results than you turning up unannounced on the doorstep like a resentful Mary Poppins, or seething silently because the O.G. is taking over the entire world, and all you can see in the future is awkward, begrudging Christmas visits while your beloved grandchild longs for the familiarity of the O.G., her primary carer. It may be that you can arrange stand-in babysitting when the O.G. fancies time off, or that the baby could come for a night at your house now and then. Bear in mind that things change, and what might seem an everlasting arrangement at the age of one might be entirely different by the time he or she is at nursery. There may be more children for a start, and then it's in everyone's interests to spread the load.

4. The 'other' grandparents are better off and buy more gifts

There are few annoyances like it – you've saved up and bought your grandchild something lovely for their birthday, then the O.G.s (the other grandparents) swoop in with a bigger, brighter, shinier version and several sackloads of extra presents besides. They're not doing it to annoy you, but because they're well off and they can. Not only is it galling, it also can feel as though you're locked in a battle of one-upmanship. One which you're destined to lose. Some parents ask grandparents to stick to a budget but there's always the chance they'll blow it because they 'couldn't resist the wooden rocking horse'. Of course, you know it's about your grandchild's enjoyment but you don't want to be thought of as the boring grandparents or, worse, the mean ones.

What To Do

You know that love is nothing to do with material goods but the average five-year-old isn't yet aware of that. She's just thrilled to have giant cuddly ponies and new party dresses. It makes sense, therefore, to speak to her mum and dad, tell them your rough budget, and ask what they'd like you to buy for her, so you don't duplicate their or the O.G.s' gifts. If they're vague, there's nothing to stop you ringing them to ask what they're getting. Don't forget that children love experiences as much, or perhaps more, than gifts, like a fancy envelope and card, which promises them a special day out (a teddy bears' picnic doesn't have to cost much) or a trip to see a pantomime with a special party tea first.

5 They're going on holiday with the other grandparents

It can be hurtful if the O.G.s regularly go on holiday with your son or daughter's family. They may be 'helping with the kids' but it's easy to feel left out if you're not invited, perhaps because it's long been a family tradition, you're the step-gran, or they're the ones who hired the house.

If it's a one-off it's unlikely you'll mind too much but if every holiday sees them jaunting off to the O.G.s' South of France hideaway chateau, it's no wonder you might feel shoved out.

What To Do

This is a rare case where actually speaking up can be useful. Telling your son or daughter, 'We know you're going to France, but we'd love to spend a bit of holiday time with you this year,' opens up a conversation – the key is not to sound accusatory. They're allowed to go on holiday with whomever they like. But tell them you'd love to see them both and the baby and that might mean a weekend booked in, or at least an overnight visit or two. Saying nothing, by contrast, can lead to resentment, martyrdom and irritation all round.

⑥ You just don't get along with the other grandparents

Just because your child has chosen to start a family with theirs, it doesn't mean you'll automatically like them. Of course, it's lovely if you form a friendship and can enjoy time all together with the grandkids but it doesn't always happen like that, particularly if you find them snobbish, rude or difficult in any way. What's worse still is if you don't agree with their child-care policies, and you're convinced that they're either spoiling them, or being too harsh. You don't want to fall out but it's hard not to say something when the baby comes back stippled with nappy rash and sucking on a stick of rock.

What To Do

Say nothing. Ever. This is a matter for the parents, not you. The only exception to this rule is if you're aware of something the parents are not, which you know would upset them but even then, it's hard not to sound like the class sneak, dobbing in a third-former for smoking. So say nothing, unless you're convinced that actual child welfare is at stake. (NB, you may not like it, but a stick of rock will not kill a child, unless they try to eat it all at once.)

And if you hate them because they're just not very nice – button it. They come as a package with your son- or daughter-in-law, and while you can subtly avoid them where possible, if you're required to play nice at family gatherings, it's better for your grandchildren if you at least pretend to get along.

7 It's always a big family gathering – you'd love some individual time with the baby

People with big families tend to get all the socializing done in one hit, to avoid weeks of clearing teacups and buying fancy pastries. But if you're not living locally, that can mean you only get to see the grandchildren when there's twelve other people clustering round the cot like a re-enactment of *Rosemary's Baby*, and your cuddling time is limited to three minutes before the relations' pass-the-parcel recommences. It's disappointing and it's hard to feel special as a grandparent when you're ninth in the queue.

What To Do

Remember that babies don't stay babies for ever. It might be hard to get dedicated time with the baby now, but as your grandchild gets older, the queue will reduce – there's not going to be a huge family gathering every other week when the 'unbelievably cute' stage has passed. In the meantime, directly offer help, rather than inviting yourself round – a few hours of babysitting to give the parents time to sleep can be worth a lot more than an afternoon drinking tea and chatting to other in-laws desperate to get their hands on the kid. Offer firmly; if it's a no, accept it, and don't moan – once your grandchild can talk on the phone and Skype, they will know exactly who you are.

I wasn't sure about my son-in-law's parents at first – they are a lot better off than us, quite upper-middle class, and I felt a bit intimidated. I felt as though they could give our granddaughter, Sasha, a lot more than we could, both in terms of time, because they're retired, and financial support. But as she got older, it became obvious that she got different things from visiting both of us: they tend to do more 'formal' things with Sasha, who's now seven, like museums and days out, whereas she loves coming to our house because we bake cakes and watch *Strictly Come Dancing* together. I now think it's great for her to have those different experiences available to her. The in-laws and us probably won't ever have a lot in common, but we all love Sasha, so that's what brings us together as a family.

Karen Ellis, 54

THINGS TO REMEMBER ABOUT THE OTHER GRANDMA

- Jealousy is a pointless emotion because there's nothing you can do about it

- Your grandchild just wants to be loved and the more of it there is around, the more balanced, happy and stable he or she will grow up

- Competing over gifts or money is a huge waste of time

- Buy what your grandchild needs, or what you can afford, and know that's more than good enough

- You don't have to be best friends with the O.G. but you do both have a major shared interest, which should ease communication between you

- If she's seeing more of your grandchild now, remember that times change and accept that you'll get your turn

---

It's entirely possible to navigate a good relationship, or at least a manageable one, with the O.G. But before we move on to the exciting bit where the baby gets born there's one more issue to resolve. What happens if you really think the other grandparents are not doing the job right when it comes to looking after your precious grandchild? Do you shut up or speak up, despite knowing that your intervention could cause a huge family rift?

It very much depends on what you perceive the failings to be. If you happen to find out that the O.G. is slipping

I was shocked when my six-year-old grandson told me that his other Nanna, Helen, had allowed him to go to the local shop alone, which involved crossing a busy main road. I asked him if his mummy knew, and he didn't seem sure. I agonized a bit over whether to say anything, but I truly believe it's too dangerous for a little boy to visit that shop by himself, so I rang my son, and, trying not to sound accusatory, asked if they were OK with it. He was surprised it had happened, and said he'd have a word with Helen about it. It turned out she'd watched him from the doorway but I still felt uneasy about it, and glad I'd brought it up. She's agreed to wait till he's a bit older before he does it again, and I hope there are no hard feelings.

Annette Parkinson, 73

your three-year-old grandchild sweets when the parents have a strict 'no sugar' policy, or it transpires that they let her have a day off school when she had a faked tummy ache, you would be a massive sneak to say anything at all to the parents, and would frankly deserve short shrift – a bit of indulgence won't harm anyone, and kids are very savvy when it comes to working out what is and isn't OK.

But if you think their well-being or safety are genuinely in danger, you have to speak up. A grandparent who is developing dementia, for instance, may not show many outward signs but if you suspect they're not fully present when your grandchild is in their care, it's high time to mention your concerns to the parents.

And if they take a particularly old-fashioned approach to discipline and smacks are a possibility, or they have designated a 'naughty step' and you just don't agree with it, then an open discussion with the parents, where you suggest that you all adhere to the same discipline code across every home, is crucial. Ultimately, parents set the agenda for what is and isn't allowed. All grandparents break the rules at their peril.

Family relationships become even more important when grandchildren are born, so it's in everybody's interests to moderate their behaviour and check what's OK with the parents. If you don't like the other family members, so be it, but they're the baby's relations too. So if you can find a way to put up with their nonsense, whether it's OCD-style cleaning whenever a Lego brick is dropped on the floor, Victorian beliefs about manners, or a far-too-relaxed attitude to watching alarming 18-certificate films while the toddler plays nearby, if you can manage to express your concerns politely and with love – or simply keep them to yourself – you'll have much happier relationships all round.

CHAPTER 4

THE FIRST YEAR

❝ I wasn't sure what it meant to be a grandma – it's very different from being a mum, but it took a while to figure out my new role. ❞

Ann Harrison, 65

During the pregnancy, despite the excitement and anticipation, it's impossible to imagine what it will feel like when the baby arrives. Will you love it the way you loved your own children, or will it be a more gentle, detached kind of love? And what will be expected of you? Will you be up to scratch?

The first issue is that most new parents are a terrifying combination of nervous and controlling, like a teenager setting off for her first prom. 'I have no idea what I'm doing, don't tell me what to do,' pretty much sums it up. Add to that their passionate, overwhelming love for the new baby, with all its protective tigress power, and it's no wonder grandparents find it difficult to know exactly how to behave.

That's why it's vital to give the new family space, unless you've specifically been asked to move in to help. This is invaluable if your own child is a single parent, or their partner is working away, otherwise three's a crowd when it comes to looking after a new baby. The best thing you can do, while they learn to look after their newborn without dropping it in the bath, or putting its nappy on backwards, is to provide silent support. Let them know you're available for help and advice if they need it, but this is a time when interference will be enormously unwelcome.

INTERFERING THINGS THAT NEW GRANDMAS SHOULD **NEVER** SAY

- ☒ Isn't she a bit little for that?'
- ☒ 'I'm not sure that's how you should hold a new baby. Careful!'
- ☒ 'Surely you're breastfeeding?'
- ☒ 'I worry about those poppers catching her skin.'
- ☒ 'I've read about formula milk, she won't get the nutrients.'
- ☒ 'Oh don't play music so loud – his little ears!'

INTERFERING THINGS THAT NEW GRANDMAS **SHOULD** SAY IF CONCERNED

- ☑ 'Don't put her to sleep on her front.'
- ☑ 'Don't share a bed with the baby.'
- ☑ 'Don't get drunk and fall asleep holding her.'

All of these can be causes of cot death and though most parents will be all too aware, if the ones you know are not you need to tell them. Nicely.

Everything else is up to them, including how long the baby sleeps for, what he or she eats and wears. So even if your three-week-old granddaughter turns up wearing an appallingly tasteless Babygro that reads 'Daddy's little squirt' with a picture of a sperm (yes, this exists, unfortunately), it's best if you simply assume it was a terrible joke present from a work colleague and that she was dressed in it because she'd been sick down everything else. Ditto flammable nylon tutus, stretchy headbands that make her look like Liza Minnelli, T-shirts for punk bands the baby doesn't know exist, and ridiculous rapper-style tracksuits and miniature Nike Airs. Yes, it's embarrassing to take your beloved grandchild for a spin in the pram when he's dressed like Jay-Z, but it's not your choice. Although some grandparents do secretly keep a cache of clothes at their house to put on the baby when they look after them, rather than endure the hideous fashion meltdown that furnishes the child's usual wardrobe. But that would be snobbish and unnecessary. Except perhaps in the case of the offensive baby-gro mentioned above.

Yes, it's interfering but sometimes it's hard to draw a distinction between how you behaved as a parent and how you expect your own son or daughter to behave towards their child. The bottom line is, they are not you and if you want to play a significant part in your grandchild's life, the best thing you can do is ban yourself from making 'helpful' suggestions based on what you did 30 years ago.

I was there for Ruby's birth, and it was truly one of the most wonderful moments of my life. My daughter was exhausted, and straight after Ruby was born, overwhelmed with love and intending to help, I held out my arms for the baby. Her husband, James, snapped, 'I haven't even held her yet!' and virtually scooped her from the nurse's arms. I felt awful, and it was a real wake-up call that as a grandparent, it doesn't matter how much love you feel, the parents come first; the baby is their responsibility, ultimately, and your role as a grandparent is backup, not front-line duties.

Elizabeth Donnelly, 70

Raising a child is a powerful biological instinct and most adults don't make too bad a job of it. If they love their child, they're 75 per cent of the way there. The other 25 per cent usually comes down to trial and error. But if you insist on correcting their parenting, you will only drive a wedge between you and your family. Of course you know better, you've already done it. But if you make it a rule that nine times out of ten you'll wait to be asked, and on the tenth, you may gently suggest an alternative approach, you won't go far wrong. It also helps enormously if you couch your advice in terms of an anecdote. So ban the words 'should' and 'shouldn't' – as in 'Shouldn't she have a blanket over that pram?' and instead say, 'I remember when you were little and wouldn't sleep, I'd always put you in the car seat and drive you round the block.' Your child is a lot more likely to listen and appreciate the suggestion than if you say, 'She's never going to go to sleep with that racket from the TV downstairs.'

Gentle suggestions that might be useful when the parents are at their wits' end:

1 THE BABY WON'T SLEEP

- ◆ **GO FOR A RIDE** – Put him in a car seat and drive him about.

- ◆ **PLAY CLASSICAL MUSIC** – Mozart has been proven to promote relaxation in babies' brains.

- ◆ **ROUTINE** – After four months, if sleep still isn't happening, try consistency – put the baby to bed at the same time every night, with the same routine. If she cries, go in and soothe her, lay her back down, retreat, and keep doing it, night after night, until it clicks that she's supposed to sleep. That fortnight may be a hell of crying, insomnia and guilt. After that, most babies finally grasp how sleep works, to their parents' utter delight.

◆ **CRANIAL OSTEOPATHY** – in dire cases when sleep is a forgotten luxury, a cranial osteopath may be able to gently realign the baby's neck bones and skull, which can be compressed after a difficult birth.

2 THE BABY WON'T STOP CRYING

This is perhaps the most upsetting thing for parents so sage advice can be very welcome.

◆ **TRY SWADDLING** – wrapping the baby tightly in a blanket can replicate the feeling of being safe in the womb. Wrap firmly but gently (YouTube videos will show you how) and place him on his back.

◆ **RHYTHMIC ROCKING** – again, he'll recall his time in the womb as he's rocked from side to side but this works best on a shoulder, rather than in a rocking cradle as many babies shriek louder when their whole environment suddenly starts pitching like a ship in a gale. Gentle swaying against a warm body, however, can work wonders.

◆ **WHITE NOISE** – several iPhone apps such as iDream offer a 'white noise' app that drowns out random sounds. Or try various ones, such as 'river' or 'tropical jungle'. However, be aware that if the baby becomes reliant on it to sleep that may not work long-term.

◆ **SUCKING** – again, be wary of creating an essential 'comfort object' (which can be lost, three years later, amid howls of grief). But in desperate times, a soft blanket or a dummy can help to soothe a baby with its familiar smell and taste.

 3 ◆ **THE BABY WON'T FEED**

◆ This is first a question for the health visitor – if the baby is failing to put weight on, or is showing signs of distress and illness, then a visit to the doctor is vital.

◆ If it's simply the case that she doesn't like bottles, or she doesn't take enough milk, patience, as you wake to feed her a bit more, and a bit more, is usually the answer.

◆ Some babies are allergic to cow's milk – suggest this could be checked, but again, interfering is never welcome, so avoid bossiness.

◆ If she's weaned, and hardly eats solids, she may be one of the many children who responds dramatically to tastes she doesn't like. It can take up to fifteen tries to get a child to warm to a particular taste, and most very small children hate anything with a strong, spicy, bitter or umami taste, so if she's being fed olive tapenade on rosemary crackers, that might explain her aversion. But a small child eating the same thing every day won't be the case for ever so don't make a huge fuss if she'll only ingest mashed potato and peas for a month.

◆ If she's suddenly gone off food, it could be a bug.

◆ If she eats perfectly well at home, but won't eat for you, it's probably a simple case of unfamiliarity. It's frustrating, but try to keep mealtimes as consistent as possible, serve foods that she knows and likes, and if she's really not having it, give up until later. No healthy baby will starve to death in a few hours.

◆ Never try to force food in when they're refusing to eat. You'll only succeed in turning mealtimes into a battleground – so bribes, threats and insistence are all a very bad idea. Just put the spoon aside, introduce some new activity, and try again later.

A WORD ABOUT BREASTFEEDING

The 'breast is best' campaign did wonders to convince women that they should breastfeed their babies, and pack them full of immunity, vitamins and lifelong joy.

Unfortunately, it also went a long way to make plenty of women feel inadequate, bad mothers, simply because they struggled to breastfeed, it was agony, or the baby wouldn't take enough milk and was wasting away while they pumped miserably for days and produced not enough for a stray cat.

Hence, sometimes new mothers decide that bottle feeding is the answer because it's consistent, fast, and means the baby gets enough nutrients all in one hit, while the dad (and grandma) can also be part of the bonding process.

And ultimately, however the baby is fed, as long as she's not having salt and vinegar crisps crushed up and stuffed into her mouth, or being given liquidized lamb vindaloo in her beaker, the bottom line is, it is none of your business. So any well-meaning hinting about what you've heard regarding the benefits of breastfeeding, or little worries over her intake of processed baby meals, or fears that powdered milk will render her helplessly weak and undernourished – keep it to yourself. The baby will be fine but this is a very sensitive issue and criticism will not be welcome. Particularly not when your daughter/in-law is suffering from raging mastitis. Never has the phrase 'when in doubt, say nowt' been more useful.

> I did worry when my daughter said she wasn't going to breastfeed. She planned to go back to work within a few months, and she said she wanted to get the baby used to a bottle, so her childminder could feed her. I was quite cross – I didn't think she had the baby's best interests at heart, and I said so. I wish I hadn't, it got me nowhere, and it caused a sharp exchange of words, where she accused me of interfering. I suppose I was, and in retrospect, even though I'd rather my granddaughter was breastfed, I do understand that it's not my place to say so.
>
> *Elizabeth Donnelly, 70*

FINDING YOUR ROLE

Once you've nailed 'not interfering' – and let's face it, you may never quite manage that (you just have to learn to do it subtly) – you will need to know exactly what your role entails.

Are you going to be the sort of gran who shows up unexpectedly with shopping bags full of clothes for the baby, or the sort who carefully plans every visit with fair warning on both sides, and would never buy the baby a gift unless you know exactly where it's going to go, and that the parents will welcome it?

Will you track every milestone of the baby's life, or just pop up every few months to assess progress? And how can you negotiate the role you hope to have, while keeping the rest of the family happy?

Useful questions to ask yourself:

- ### HOW MUCH TIME DO I HAVE?

  Are you retired and happy to swap gentle volunteering for childminding, work part-time but have other commitments on days off, or in full-time work, with only your precious weekends for cramming in hobbies, friends and relaxation? It's essential that you're realistic about what you can offer, timewise.

- ### HOW MUCH ENERGY DO I HAVE?

  Being a fit 55 is very different from being a tired 85 (or even a fit and energetic 85). As you get older, health becomes a bigger issue and while you might feel perfectly fine, looking after a small child is exhausting. If you're also trying to fit it around other commitments, you might end up compromising your health, and being unable to keep to arrangements you've made. Don't agree a childcare plan without at least a trial week, to see how tiring you find the suggested arrangement.

- ### HOW MUCH SPACE DO I HAVE?

  If you have a big house, it might make sense to spend time there with your grandchild when you're looking after them, particularly if you have a bigger garden, or a spare room that can be turned into the baby's room. If you live in a tiny flat, however, with a low balcony, a steep staircase, and sharp corners everywhere, you'd be better off visiting the baby's own home when it comes to grandma duties. Of course, this is ultimately up to the parents but most won't object to a break from crying.

● HOW MUCH CONFIDENCE DO I HAVE?

It's assumed that grandmas just know stuff: how to bath a baby, how to warm a bottle, how to jiggle a crying newborn over one shoulder and knit a bonnet with the other hand. But when it's been 35 years since the last time you forensically detected what caused a burst of wild sobbing, or pushed a pram across a busy road, it's no wonder you may feel a little intimidated. New parents may simply expect that you know exactly what you're doing, but some things have to be relearned. There's no point in pretending to be more confident than you are, and no shame at all in admitting that it may take you a while to get up to speed. Just as some people refuse to drive on the motorway, despite having a perfectly good driving licence, some grandparents would prefer not to be left in sole charge of the baby. That doesn't mean you can't offer support while the parents hover at a safe distance.

● HOW MUCH SUPPORT DO I HAVE?

There's a big difference between being a lone grand-parent, due to divorce or bereavement, and being 'grandparents' where you can both share the child-care, offer different types of care, and one can make cups of tea while the other gets up at 3 a.m. to do the night feed. If you're alone, you may find you're keen to spend even more time with a grandchild or you might find that you get more tired, because there's no one else to help you out. This is where honesty is again vital – let your family know what you feel able to do and if they boldly insist that 'You'll be fine!' (read: 'We're dying for a night out, get a grip!'), just let them know, gently but firmly, that you really don't feel secure being left in sole charge and that you'll need a while longer to practise with supervision.

● HOW MUCH MONEY DO I HAVE?

This is not an irrelevant question, despite the fact that love should conquer all when it comes to grand-children. The truth is that plenty of grandparents do agree a financial contribution to look after grand-children regularly. If that doesn't sit easily, there's the question of expenses. Are you happy to purchase baby food, nappies, bedding, tickets for days out, extra toys, and everything else that comes with the day-to-day care of a baby or toddler? Then there's the extra transport costs, and the presents for birthdays and Christmas. Even if you're not going to be a regular carer for the baby, you may want to think about a budget because if your son or daughter is expecting a new Bugaboo pram for Christmas, and you're thinking vaguely about a few Babygros, it's better if nobody ends up feeling used or disappointed. Money is a minefield to discuss with family but even if you don't want to bring it up in conversation, it makes sense to have an idea in your own mind of what you can and can't spend, at least partly so you don't get carried away with excitement, and sink into debt buying silk christening gowns and Harrods nursing chairs.

HOW TO HAVE THE CONVERSATION

Whatever your answers to the above questions, generally speaking, it's a lot easier to talk about your plans, hopes and expectations directly after you've listened to the parents' own. Never go steaming in, laying out your terms: 'I thought Annabel could come once a week on a Friday night, and I'll get a sterilizer, but if you want to send frozen breast milk . . .' This will almost certainly result in the parents feeling coerced, and either resentfully compelled to agree, or send them straight to refusal without passing go, because 'the trouble with Mum is, she never listens'. So start any discussion by asking what they'd like to happen, then go from there.

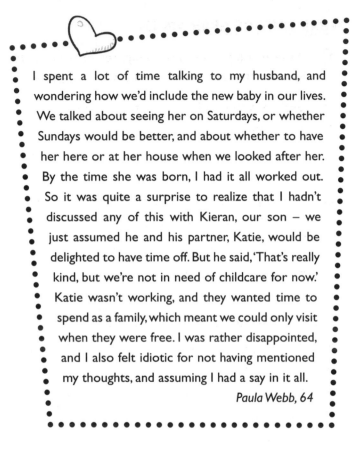

I spent a lot of time talking to my husband, and wondering how we'd include the new baby in our lives. We talked about seeing her on Saturdays, or whether Sundays would be better, and about whether to have her here or at her house when we looked after her. By the time she was born, I had it all worked out. So it was quite a surprise to realize that I hadn't discussed any of this with Kieran, our son – we just assumed he and his partner, Katie, would be delighted to have time off. But he said, 'That's really kind, but we're not in need of childcare for now.' Katie wasn't working, and they wanted time to spend as a family, which meant we could only visit when they were free. I was rather disappointed, and I also felt idiotic for not having mentioned my thoughts, and assuming I had a say in it all.

Paula Webb, 64

The truth is, it's lovely if the parents listen to you but you're barking up entirely the wrong tree if you think it's a given. And if you're still not sure what kind of grandma you want to be – hands on, hands off, or somewhere in between – here's a quick quiz to help you decide.

WHAT SORT OF GRAN AM I?

1 It's late at night and your daughter rings in a panic because the baby won't stop crying. Do you say:

a. 'Perhaps you should try ignoring her for a bit.'

b. 'I'm getting dressed. I'll be round in ten minutes.'

c. 'Try another bottle and then play Mozart, it worked with you.'

d. 'Just pop her in the car, and drive her about. I'm here if you want to drop in.'

2 You don't like what your grandchild is wearing. Do you:

a. Ignore it – it's no skin off your nose

b. Change him into something nicer – then back again by hometime

c. Ask if you can buy him a jumper, in case he gets cold

d. Add a witty strawberry-shaped knitted hat to his ensemble

3 The baby's had a cold for a week. Do you suggest:

a. Nothing – it'll get better of its own accord

b. Swaddling, infant paracetamol, nasal drops

c. A quick visit to the doctor just in case

d. That you can look after him to give his mum a break

4 It's your granddaughter's birthday. Do you buy her:

a. A voucher

b. Several carefully chosen items you think she'd love

c. A new cot because her old one was second-hand and it worries you

d. A dress and a cake

5 You're babysitting for the afternoon. Is your chosen activity:

a. To spend time with the grandchild. No more than that

b. Park, sleep, tea, cuddle, bath

c. Playing in the living room, followed by singing and toys

d. Visiting a friend of yours, a bit of shopping, maybe a cafe

MOSTLY A: **HANDS-OFF GRAN**

You're the kind of gran who does best when you're not required to put masses of time in. You love your grandchild dearly, but you don't feel compelled to spend every minute with him or her. You'll do best as a gran with scheduled visits, plenty of warning, and a capacity to offer advice when asked, even if you're not quite sure of the answers. A little willingness to discuss the minutiae of child care would go a long way.

MOSTLY B: **HANDS-ON GRAN**

You are the gran who keeps on giving – no task is too large, no steaming nappy too full, no 4 a.m. panic call too late. You are poised like a ninja, ready to swoop in bearing wet wipes, sterilizers and scratch mittens at a moment's notice.

And while the exhausted new parents may be endlessly grateful, there's a danger you'll burn out before your grandchild hits the three-month mark. Try to take a step back and trust that the parents will work it out occasionally – you'll need some energy for the toddler years.

MOSTLY C: **PERFECT GRAN**

You are Perfect Gran, determined to do everything right – from the correct feeding regime to the perfect temperature to careful educational play at consistent times. That means your precious grandchild is never in danger in your loving care but it also means you'll lie awake worrying about sniffles, rashes, squeaks, itches and sneezes. Your commitment is admirable, but try to remember that most children survive babyhood, and if she eats a raisin off the floor, or tumbles off a rug, she probably won't be scarred for life.

MOSTLY D: **CHILLED GRAN**

You see no reason why the baby can't fit into your life. You've probably had tons of experience of juggling babies, work, socializing and cooking, all at the same time. You're not afraid to get stuck in, but you remain unfazed by the glitches and hitches of babyhood. Crying is never the end of the world (even when it's the baby's dad), and an alarming swelling, to you, is nearly always teething and not meningitis. Remember though, that while this may be second nature to you, the new parents may find every tiny hiccup alarming, so don't automatically dismiss their concerns.

AND FINALLY . . .

Negotiating your role, working out what's interfering and what's just helpful steering, is tricky, and don't forget that circumstances constantly change, and what may work when the baby's two months old may be redundant by the time he or she is one. You will make mistakes, you may offend your son or daughter by interfering, or messing with arrangements, or changing your mind, or putting on the wrong nappy, or holding the baby upside down. It may require some discussion, or you might decide to say nothing and yourself be guided entirely by the needs of the new parents. And if you disapprove of their child-care practices? Unless the child is in mortal danger (unlikely), remind yourself that babies have thrived against all odds, living under hedges and in dresser drawers, and fed on scraps of stale bread. Though it's unlikely to come to that. Besides, any dispute will be resolved sooner or later because it's your grandchild, and you love them. And that will be the case no matter what sort of grandmother you decide to be, and which role you feel most comfortable with.

CHAPTER 5

CHILDCARE AND CASH

❝ I had sleepless nights over the money issue – I didn't want to ask for any, but I couldn't afford not to. ❞

Sheila Farnham, 60

Half of parents depend on the 'informal' childcare offered by grandparents. 'Informal' generally means you don't get paid, or at least, that you're on expenses only. Added to that, grans who look after their grandchildren regularly are also more likely to be younger (in their 40s and 50s), have a job, and likely to be managing on a low income. In the UK alone, there are around 14 million grandparents – so that's a lot of childcare. Perhaps it seems a bit brutal to reduce the love you feel for your grandchild to cold, hard cash. But just as parents need money to pay for the baby, there's a good chance you do too, particularly if you're among the many thousands of low-income households. Because baby paraphernalia doesn't come cheap, and if you're putting in the hours, you're also putting on the nappies, and stuffing the jars of pricey, organic mango puree into their ever-open mouths.

When my son's first baby was born, he and his wife asked if I would consider being Colm's carer when they went back to work full-time. I agonized over it. The pros were: I lived very close by, they trusted me 100 per cent, and I could obviously be flexible about looking after him at my house and theirs. After a few sleepless nights, I gave in my notice at work – I was a receptionist for a big company, which I enjoyed, but this seemed much more important.

I agreed that I'd just take expenses from my son. I didn't even like asking for that, but I was taking a big financial hit by giving up my job, and my husband and I agreed we'd dig into our savings to make up the shortfall. It went fine for a year but when Colm was 18 months old, Sally was made redundant and the only job she could get in her field was 50 miles away. They moved to be nearer her work, and although I understood, I was devastated, partly because I missed Colm so much, but also because I couldn't get my old job back and now I was effectively retired, with nothing to do, at just 56. I try to visit whenever I can, but if I could have the time back, I wouldn't give up work, I'd go part-time at most.

Cathy Biggar, 58

And if you're giving up work to become the primary carer for your grandchild, that's a whole new minefield involving tax, benefits, pensions, employment rights, health and safety issues, and quite probably a meeting with the security head of the UN before you can even begin to change a nappy. So working out what you can offer, what it means, emotionally and financially, and what happens if it all goes horribly wrong (it almost certainly won't but just in case . . .) is crucial.

Giving up work is a big decision and as Cathy (opposite) discovered, unfortunately, there's no guarantee that your new role as a childminder will last for ever.

A few useful questions to consider before you cry, 'Of course I will!' and hand in your notice:

■ CAN I AFFORD TO GIVE UP WORK?

Your work almost certainly provides an income which you need. Giving up may mean sacrifices.

■ CAN I GO PART-TIME?

If you work full-time, part-time could be an option but you may find having two jobs very tiring (because looking after a baby is a job and then some).

■ WHAT IF IT DOESN'T WORK OUT, AND I WANT MY JOB BACK?

Check your status in the company; you could even consider taking a sabbatical in certain careers, but it could only be on the understanding that you'll return. This option may be feasible for temporary childcare.

■ WHAT WILL HAPPEN TO MY BENEFITS?

If you don't work full-time but are on sickness pay, or other benefits, taking on a childcare role could have an impact. Check online if you think this could affect you or contact the relevant authorities or a financial adviser.

■ WHAT IF I MISS MY JOB?

It may seem selfish to prefer your old job to golden hours of grandchild joy but the truth is childcare is hard, grinding work, and a job you enjoy means a ready-made social life, an income, and a reason to leave the house. So be very aware of what you're giving up.

■ WHAT IF THERE'S MORE THAN ONE?

Looking after one grandchild is tiring but doable. But what happens if another one comes along? Can you sign up for that, and if not, does that mean they have separate carers?

■ WHAT IF THEY MOVE AWAY AND I'M LEFT WITH NO JOB AND NO GRANDCHILD TO MIND?

This is the worst of all worlds and it can happen. So if you are going to commit to the role, it can be wise to find out if the family are willing to commit to staying put in return. Don't forget that at two or three, your grandchild may start playgroup or nursery so by its nature, it's not a full-time role that lasts for ever.

What you answer to all of these questions will determine whether you're suited to a role as a full- or part-time child carer, and if you feel you're not, due to other commitments, financial needs, practical issues or health reasons, the worst thing you can do is say 'yes' when you mean 'no'. This is a situation built entirely on trust so if you can't be honest at the outset, it's unlikely to get easier.

Of course, turning down the glorious offer of endless days with the little one won't be easy but rather than saying, 'No, I can't,' it'll go down a whole lot better if you can explain why and to avoid attempts at persuasion, add, 'I've thought about it very hard, we've discussed it endlessly, and I just don't think it's the fairest option for me, you or the baby.' The tone of this discussion should be firm yet loving and you must be willing to explain your reasons at length, so everyone understands exactly where they stand. If you say, 'I'll have her whenever I can,' that can be interpreted as 'every time of day or night that you're not sleeping or commuting'. If you say, however, 'How about one morning a week – Wednesday is good for me,' it leaves no one in any doubt regarding your intentions. Yes, they may be condemned to forking out for childcare but so are millions of parents. And having a gran who lives nearby doesn't make free childcare a God-given right.

But if you're saying yes, that's a different thing altogether. And that's where the negotiations really start in earnest.

Full-time childcare is a huge commitment but if the parents are going part-time, it can be a perfect compromise. Either way, that's when it's vital to decide if – or what – to charge.

REASONS TO CHARGE

❋ You've given up work and genuinely need the money

❋ You're providing a full-time driving, feeding and entertainment service

❋ You feel it makes things more formal, and this way nobody feels exploited, plus the parents get to stipulate what they want, as you are effectively working for them

REASONS NOT TO CHARGE

❋ They're your grandchildren and it doesn't feel right to equate care with money

❋ You don't need the money, but the parents do

❋ You're caring for the children in their own house, so it's not costing you anything

I agreed to be the full-time carer for my twin granddaughters. I knew it was a huge commitment but I was planning to retire soon, and I've always been a doer – I hated the idea of drifting around with no purpose to my days. So when they asked me, I leapt at the chance. I didn't want money, as I've got a good pension. My husband was very unsure; he loves the girls too, but thought it would be a huge task, and very disruptive. But I'd had three children pretty close together, and I felt sure I was up to it. I gave my notice in at work, and within a month, they were round at my house from 8.30 a.m. to 6 p.m. If I'm honest, I found it exhausting at first; my husband helped but I was the main carer. It also meant I needed weekends to recharge, so we didn't do any family stuff then, which meant I hardly ever saw my daughter and the twins together. Two years on, they're so rewarding, we have an incredible bond, and I've remembered skills I'd forgotten I had, including cake-baking, painting and bear hunting. They start nursery school next year, and I will only have them two afternoons a week. It'll be more relaxing but I'll miss them so much.

Ali Nordstrom, 66

And if you do want to be paid, this is where it gets tricky. Because although you can be paid expenses for looking after the baby for things like nappies, driving costs, equipment or food, if you're going to charge an actual fee, that means that at the time of writing, in the UK you need to be registered as a childminder. Which means you'll need basic training, and will need to at least sometimes care for another child (who isn't related), be registered, have a security check and public liability insurance, and have your premises inspected.

Given the complexities, the vast majority of grandparents agree to an informal 'expenses' arrangement, though it's still a good idea to keep a tab of costs and agree a regular payment date so you don't spend your life saying, 'I hate to remind you, but I bought that entrance ticket to the zoo two years ago . . .'

It's also the case that many grandparents wouldn't dream even of charging expenses. If parents are willing to drop off all the equipment the baby needs, and you don't mind making up the shortfall now and then, this can be a very wise option and avoids any resentment, financial complications, or expectation on either side because as a grandparent, you have far more flexibility to say 'no' than you do as an employee.

THINGS YOU'LL NEED

If you're looking after a baby full- or even part-time, while certain items can be shuttled back and forth (like the increasingly filthy comfort blanket that you must NEVER wash because you will destroy all the reassuring scent with a burst of lemon-fresh fabric softener) it makes sense to gather a selection of key items in your own home. These might include:

* **A COT AND TWO SETS OF BEDDING:** travel cots are all very well, but unless you're tight on space, they're a faff to put up and take down every few nights. And if you've got the space, you may as well have a proper cot that won't give you lumbago when you try to put the baby down into it.

* **DISHES AND BOTTLES:** improvising with your own china and giant-sized adult forks is unwise with a baby who's just learning to eat. Invest in some Thomas the Tank Engine/Peppa Pig bowls and little cutlery to encourage eating.

* **A CHANGING MAT/STATION:** makes it a lot easier than trying to change a slippery baby on a sofa.

* **NAPPIES:** always have a stock of your own – if you don't, they will forget one day, and that means a walk in the rain to the shop with a squalling baby in a damp nappy.

❋   **BABY WIPES:** for everything.

❋   **A FEW CHANGES OF CLOTHES:** not just because you like your own taste in baby clothes better than your daughter-in-law's but more because it's almost certainly that day the baby will explode at one end or the other at least three times and washing machines don't work that fast.

❋   **INFANT PARACETAMOL AND A BABY THERMOMETER**

❋   **A TOY BOX:** don't go mad on toys – for most under 3's, playing with leaves, making cakes, drawing with crayons and generally following you about like a duckling will be entertaining enough. But if your grandchild is spending a lot of time with you, toys and books are very useful indeed. Buy them from charity shops – a quick wipe and they'll be as good as new. Plus you can then have a high turnover to keep them amused.

❋   **DVDS:** you may disapprove but sometimes a Disney film is nothing short of a godsend.

THINGS YOU DON'T NEED

◆ **A BOTTLE STERILIZER:** it takes up huge amounts of worktop or cupboard space, and a pan of boiling water and sterilizing solution will do just as well.

◆ **ANOTHER PRAM:** Again, space-eating and very expensive. Just use the parents' one and if parents are dropping your grandchild off by car, they can drop the pram too.

◆ **A FULLY DECORATED ROOM:** don't feel you have to clear out your office or spare room and entirely redecorate for the baby. He or she will be perfectly happy tucked into a corner of the living room, or your bedroom, where they can hear and see people nearby.

◆ **A BABY WALKER:** they take up a lot of space, are potentially hazardous (being the runaway trains of the baby world) and aren't recommended for a baby to be in for more than 20 minutes. A playpen is a better bet if you need to put them in something.

PART-TIMERS

If you're on call for caring during the holidays only, or as and when, it can be difficult to plan. Any ad-hoc arrangement, which often happens if a parent is self-employed or freelance, and may have to work at short notice, or go away overnight, can be tricky to navigate if you're never quite sure when you'll be needed. And when the children get to nursery, you may be needed in the school holidays, but not at other times, even when you've got used to being Gran On Call, morning noon and night.

Negotiating the times you'll be looking after the grandchildren can work perfectly well as long as you're happy with flexibility, but this won't work so well if you work part-time or have a whole raft of commitments.

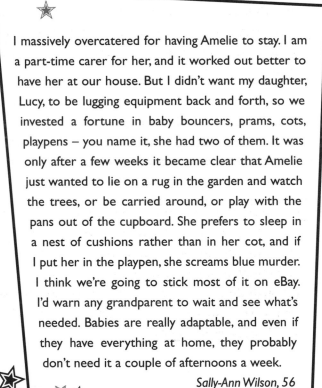

I massively overcatered for having Amelie to stay. I am a part-time carer for her, and it worked out better to have her at our house. But I didn't want my daughter, Lucy, to be lugging equipment back and forth, so we invested a fortune in baby bouncers, prams, cots, playpens – you name it, she had two of them. It was only after a few weeks it became clear that Amelie just wanted to lie on a rug in the garden and watch the trees, or be carried around, or play with the pans out of the cupboard. She prefers to sleep in a nest of cushions rather than in her cot, and if I put her in the playpen, she screams blue murder. I think we're going to stick most of it on eBay. I'd warn any grandparent to wait and see what's needed. Babies are really adaptable, and even if they have everything at home, they probably don't need it a couple of afternoons a week.

Sally-Ann Wilson, 56

Some possible solutions to childcare problems are:

* Share childcare with your partner. If you're both able-bodied and reasonably energetic, there's no reason why you shouldn't take turns looking after the children, plus it gives them a wider experience, doing different things with Granny and Grandad.

* Share childcare with a registered childminder. The parents may be wary of putting their baby into 'formal' childcare and the cost is an issue, but if you can arrange that the childminder does mornings, for instance, and you can collect your grandchild at lunchtime, it may work out perfectly.

* Share the childcare with the other grandparents, or aunties and uncles. This may be the best arrangement of all – everyone gets a certain amount of freedom, and the baby gets to spend lots of time with people it knows and loves.

* Organize flexi-time. Some employers may be willing to let you work different hours to fit round your childcare commitments, or work from home – the best option if you don't know when you'll be needed. (Though don't try to work while you're looking after the baby. Not because any harm will come to her, simply because it's impossible.)

Many – if not most – families manage a rolling arrangement on childminding, with no formal hours in place. Ideally, if you're doing one overnight a week, say, it works best if you stick to the same night. But if that's not possible, or you're going round to their house to look after the baby during parental night-shifts, remember it won't last for ever, and only agree to what you know you can manage, to avoid feeling exploited or just plain exhausted.

The bottom line is negotiate the childcare you're able and willing to do. And learn to accept that registered childminders are generally very nice people, who care about their charges, so if your precious grandchild does experience a little 'formal' childcare, they'll almost certainly turn out just fine.

CHAPTER 6

PLAYING BY THE RULES – OR NOT

❝ I don't always agree with my daughter's rules but I'd be insane to argue with them. ❞

Tana Lockley, 65

There is one big problem when you don't agree with the rules set by your grandchild's parents. He or she is not your child and there's nothing you can do. Sorry to be brutal but there it is. If you want a harmonious, happy relationship with the baby and its parents, the quickest way to derail that and send it crashing over a cliff straight past the signs marked 'resentment' and 'acrimony' is to criticize their rules and lifestyle choices. Because ultimately, when it comes to rules, you cannot win. You may be jam-packed with useful advice, desperate to share your hard-won wisdom and terrified the baby won't survive to its first birthday if they don't stop giving him bits of breadstick to choke on, and risking him rolling off the sofa. But saying anything at all is a minefield with only a few exceptions.

The exceptions are as follows:

* If you genuinely believe the baby will come to harm, for example, you suspect she's allergic to something such as cow's milk; or you think she's being left with someone you have very good reason not to trust.

* If you know a fact that the parents don't, not an opinion. For example, it's a fact that too much salt is dangerous for young children. So if they're mashing up stock cubes for her, step in. This is not the same as having doubts about the nutritional goodness of certain soft drinks.

* If you truly believe one of her parents is not competent, either mentally ill, abusing substances, neglectful or otherwise unable to care for the baby and keep her safe. (This does not mean 'has a glass of wine at night'.)

That's it. If you're going to question any other rules and choices that the parents make, you'd better be on very solid ground, and if you're even going to quirk your lips, roll your eyes, or sigh heavily, you should know you're risking your entire future relationship. New parents are extremely sensitive, and most will have pored over baby-care books at great length. They will also almost certainly know other parents of babies, with whom they will discuss every breath and whimper the baby makes. So unless you are specifically asked for advice, keep quiet. And even if you are, think very carefully about how you phrase it.

I admit I am a bit controlling. But I found my daughter-in-law's ways of doing things quite challenging. I am a mum of four, but she didn't ask me for advice. I constantly had to bite my lip — she'd bath the baby in a slippy bubble bath, and then try and lift her out without putting a towel round her first, so my heart was in my mouth; and she'd bang her on the back if she coughed, quite violently, I thought. Then there were the times she'd feed her bits of what we were eating at just six months and I thought it would upset her stomach. But when I did say something, I got short shrift. My son said, 'It's how we like to do things,' and I just had to shut up, for fear of harming the relationship. I'm getting used to what I see as their overly chilled-out attitude but it's tricky.

Sally Whittler, 49

The rules change, of course, as your grandchild gets older. At two, she can't go to bed after six-thirty. At 16, she's got to be in by midnight. But navigating someone else's rules, particularly when they are set by — and apply to — people you love, is very hard when you don't agree. And even if you do, the question is, how much and are you prepared to bend the rules on your own turf? There are several areas where things might go a little wrong so be aware of their reasons before you steam in, and whether your worries are based on facts or feelings.

BEDTIME

The received wisdom says that a child should be put down at the same time every night, with a nightlight, and that if this happens consistently, they will eventually learn to get themselves to sleep.

You may agree with that or you may believe that a baby should be picked up when it cries, rocked back to sleep, and fed on demand. The fact is, there is no definite consensus on what works, and what suits one set of parents and their baby may be disastrous for another. The only caveat is, official advice states that a small baby should never share the parental bed, a carer should not fall asleep holding the baby, and that it should always be laid on its back to sleep, to prevent cot death. If they're not observing this advice, speak up – gently. As far as everything else goes, there's no hard and fast rule.

THE EXCEPTION: if the baby is clearly exhausted through lack of sleep. At that point, any new parent will welcome gentle advice.

CRYING

When you're a veteran of crying babies, it can be quite easy to tell the difference between 'tired mewling' and urgent, 'I'm lying on a pin' shrieking. But for inexperienced parents, it's like learning a new language and they need time to do that. So even if they mistake 'tired' for 'hungry' and mess up feeding times, or change nappies unnecessarily when the real problem is that the baby's too hot, nothing terrible is going to happen. The only issue comes if they have a policy on picking the baby up or not because if your tried and tested method was 'controlled crying' and theirs is 'rock him every time he whimpers' – or vice versa – it may be a stretch for you to overlook all you know. It's better for the baby, however, to experience consistency, so if that's what the parents want, that's what you do.

THE EXCEPTION: if the baby is truly distressed, or the crying is accompanied by vomiting, fever or other symptoms, and you suspect illness, don't wait for them to realize, take them to the hospital.

CLOTHING AND JEWELLERY

As noted earlier, the parents' clothing rules may be very different from yours. It may be that you think your grandchildren's clothes are impractical, silly, or inappropriate: haircuts baby bangles that squash their wrists, tiny Tiffany necklaces that look tacky, or perhaps most controversial of all – pierced ears. Often, it can be a cultural issue – in the Far East and India, pierced ears are not unusual for babies and adorning their tiny limbs with jewellery is considered perfectly desirable. So before you object, be careful you're not wading into a cultural and familial minefield.

THE EXCEPTION: if something it's wearing is hurting the baby, through itching or pinching, or there's a high likelihood she's going to catch an earring on her lace frock. In which case, point this out, no parent wants their baby to be in pain.

EATING

This is where it gets tricky. All babies are different and all parents have their own beliefs about bottle- or breast-feeding, when to wean, and what to feed them. Busy mums and dads might choose to roll out a selection of jars, pots and microwaveable boxes, while you truly think that your grandchild will only thrive on a diet of kale and quinoa. Others may obsess dramatically over pureeing butternut squash, and measuring out agave nectar so their child never comes into contact with sugar; which might not be in line with your belief that a bit of chocolate can't hurt when they're kicking up a fuss in the post office queue.

There are, however, foods that are choking hazards, foods that are actively harmful to babies, and foods that are just not very nutritious. The latter won't kill them. The first two might. So in this case, if you disagree, you may have to speak up.

THE EXCEPTIONS: anything other than milk before four months. Before the baby is one, avoid honey (it contains bacteria that can cause botulism); cow's milk, because it's hard for a baby's stomach to digest its proteins; and any small, hard foods that can lodge in their throat, like sweets, meat chunks, grapes or tomatoes, which can be inhaled whole by a greedy baby. If you're worried about choking, say so, it doesn't take much time to cut up a grape.

ENTERTAINMENT

This is where the rules really come into play and as they get older, they get more complex. 'He's allowed to watch *Strictly*, but not *X Factor*, and if he's been good he can watch ten minutes of *Doctor Who*, or play on the iPad for twenty minutes, but only if it's *Night Zookeeper*, not the driving game because he gets overwrought . . .' If you're doing the babysitting, it's very tempting to overrule the 'home' rules' with your own, specially if *Downton Abbey* is on and you want to watch it.

As for toys, this is an issue that rears up at Christmas and birthdays – is she allowed a trike yet? What about a child's laptop? Are teenage dolls for five-year-olds horribly inappropriate and sexist, or excellent training in how to be a girl? And what about time online, and what programmes are permitted? There is some flexibility in this or should be. Discuss your own feelings about TV and what's OK, supervise online time, and it's likely a compromise can be reached when your grandchild is with you.

THE EXCEPTION: if your small grandchild is allowed to watch adult films and programmes at home, or spend unsupervised time online, you may need to speak up. Plenty of adult content is inappropriate, not because of swearing, which most kids either don't understand or find funny, or even sex, but because of violence, which studies suggest affects their developing brains. The same is true, if not more so, of computer games, such Grand Theft Auto – they are rated 18 for a reason, so feel free to question their access to them.

CLEANLINESS

One person's rough and tumble playing is another's washer-dryer nightmare. So if your grandchild arrives freshly cleaned and ironed, with new shoes on, and your view is that children shouldn't be gussied up like show ponies to go to the park, it's likely you'll send them back looking as if they've rolled down a mountain and swam through a river. This may be a good thing but the parents may not agree. Alternatively, you might be a big believer in the power of cleanliness – daily baths, assiduous teeth brushing and regular hair washing no matter whether water goes in the eyes or not. And the parents may be a little more relaxed about these things. Either way, if your rules on keeping clean, getting clean and staying clean don't match up, it can make for a few grumpy exchanges. Again, the ball is in the parental court here, so if you want to bake cakes and run about, keep some little aprons or overalls at your house. And if you like them to be sparkling with cleanliness, check whether you can give them a bath before bringing them home.

THE EXCEPTION: extreme mud-coverage – it's reasonable to clean any child who looks as if they've just played a rugby match in a bog.

BREAKING THE RULES

Plenty of grandparents recklessly ignore parental rules – not the sensible ones like 'put her in a car seat' or 'don't feed babies salty popcorn' – but when the children get slightly older, there's often a grandparental sense that rules are made to be broken, and that as long as they 'don't tell Mummy', it's fine. There are two schools of thought here: one is that it's not remotely fine to encourage small children to keep secrets, for obvious reasons, and that it undermines their trust in their parents, and their perception of adults as on the same side. The other is that once in a while, it does kids no harm to have a bit of a fun 'Shhh, don't tell Mum' bag of sweets when Mum said they weren't allowed, or to be permitted to watch the end of a film, and go to bed half an hour late.

The former means you will not fall out with your daughter or son because you are following their rules to the letter. But it does mean that you'll have more of a struggle as your grandchild gets older, and attempts to play you off against each other ('Mummy always lets me stay up late . . .') Because if you don't give in, you may have to deal with a tantruming, sulking, tear-sodden toddler, whose sorrows could be instantly ironed out with a second bowl of their favourite cereal or a toy. Good luck with resisting that.

On the other hand, if you do have Granny's Special Secrets – late bedtimes, sleeping in your bed when she's meant to be in her own, extra crisps and contraband sweeties – it will come back and bite you firmly on the bottom. 'Nancy says you let her have a bag of Minstrels, after I EXPRESSLY SAID . . .' 'Why is Archie claiming that he was allowed to watch late-night television and drink Coca-Cola?'

Little children – fortunately – are terrible at keeping secrets, and relying on their discretion is like telling your darkest secrets to a drunk friend on a night out and expecting it to remain under wraps. Besides which, while it may be OK to set up a culture of undermining when they're little, because it's 'doing no harm', what happens when they're ten and begging you not to tell their dad about their bad report, or 15 and asking you not to mention the arrest for graffitiing a bus?

If you set up a 'one rule at Granny's, another at home' culture, it can work as long as it's all out in the open, and they know, say, that they're allowed sweets on a Friday night when they stay with you, but not at home; or that at your house they can climb on the furniture, but at home they have to take their shoes off. Most children are quite easily able to grasp what's fair and will readily accept that different adults have different rules. But if you do this, it's essential to be consistent – cakes before breakfast can't be OK one week, and forbidden the next. So if you do allow them to break a rule, think hard about whether you want them to do it every time.

RULES YOU CAN BREAK

If you're going to break the parenting rules, here are the ones you can just about get away with:

☑ **SWEETS:** unless they're allergic, diabetic, or have shockingly bad tooth decay, a couple of sweets from toddlerhood upwards isn't going to kill them. But don't let them have the whole bag unless you want Tartrazine-fuelled madness followed by sobbing. And make them brush their teeth afterwards.

☑ **FAST FOOD:** a thorny area. Be very sure you want to go down this route because once they've tasted cheap burger and chips, they'll want it ever after. Packed with salt, additives and protein, it's drugs in food form. To be used only in emergencies.

☑ **BEDTIMES:** staying up a bit later at Granny's is manageable as long as you're dealing with the fallout of tiredness next day. Staying up all evening till they're crimson-eyed with exhaustion is not.

☑ **CLEANLINESS:** they can get away without having a bath once in a while. If they're covered in grass stains, ice cream and chocolate, at the very least wipe them down with a damp cloth and always change a baby's nappy at bedtime; if they hate having baths, you can let it slide now and then.

RULES YOU CAN'T BREAK

☒ **SWEARING:** if they can't swear at home, they can't swear at your house. And they probably shouldn't either. (And nor should you.)

☒ **RELIGIOUS/CULTURAL RULES:** you may think a no pork rule set by your Muslim daughter-in-law, or a no mixing milk and meat rule from your Jewish son-in-law is silly but it's not for you to say how they bring up their child. The same goes for vegetarians, so no slipping your grandchild a lamb chop in secret.

☒ **DISCIPLINE:** if there's a naughty step at home, there should be one at your house too, or a 'time out' area, or a tone of voice that they instantly know is a warning. By all means be more indulgent but there should be sanctions for bad behaviour, unless you've already agreed that the parents will deal with it later.

☒ **TV/COMPUTERS:** there's no point parents trying to impose discipline regarding what they can and can't watch, if all they have to do is show up at your house for a marathon of inappropriate and terrifying late-night movies.

ARE YOU A RULE-BREAKER OR A GOODY TWO SHOES GRANNY?

Not sure where you stand on the rules? Take this quick quiz to find out what sort of gran you are – rebellious relative or parental prefect?

1 **The rule is 'NO SWEETS BEFORE A MEAL'. Do you interpret this as:**

a. No fruit either – sweet foods are terrible for teeth and cause insulin crashes

b. A useful way to offer a reward 'if you eat all your fish fingers'

c. A couple of sweets won't do any harm. OK, and a chocolate bar . . .

My own mum was always breaking the rules with my two. I knew she was stuffing them with sweets whenever my back was turned, and they'd come back from staying at her house exhausted because she'd let them stay up watching musicals with her. It was good for them to have a place to go to let off steam and know they'd get away with being a bit naughty. But with my grandchildren, I try to stick to the rules 90 per cent of the time. Their parents aren't that strict, so the only times I break them are if they want a snack before tea and are starving. I just say, 'Make sure you eat your tea,' and they do. Or I'll sometimes carry the little one when she's tired, even though I know her dad thinks she should walk now. I think grandparents tend to be more patient, we have more time, so perhaps the rules don't seem as important. You have the long view, and know an extra cake or another game before bed won't really do any harm, whereas to mums and dads it can seem like a huge battle to be fought.

Karen Ellis, 54

PLAYING BY THE RULES – OR NOT

2 **The rule is 'NO SLEEPING IN GRANNY'S BED'. Does this mean:**

a. If she comes in during the night, you'll lead her back to her own bed, and tuck her in

b. Only after a nightmare or a bed-wetting episode

c. Only if it's the middle of the night and you're half asleep

3 **The rule is 'HALF AN HOUR OF CHILDREN'S TELEVISION AND NO MORE'. Is that:**

a. More than enough

b. Not enough time for you to find out what happens at the end of *Frozen*

c. A flexible piece of string depending how busy you are

4 **The rule is 'BAD BEHAVIOUR MEANS TIME ON THE NAUGHTY STEP'. Are you:**

a. Fine with that and it's a very useful warning

b. Happy to use it as a threat but not to actually put it into practice

c. What naughty step? Distraction works better. 'Look! A squirrel!'

5 **The rule is 'ONE STORY BEFORE BEDTIME'. Do you:**

a. Read one story, turn on the nightlight, quietly leave

b. Read two stories. As long as they're shortish

c. Keep going until they fall asleep. It's nice to have an audience

MOSTLY A: **GOOD GRANNY**

You're determined to do everything by the book and if that means prioritizing the parents' needs – and your relationship with them – over your grandchild's desires, that's what you'll do. You're adult-oriented, rational, and don't see the point in challenging other people's rules, even if you don't agree with them. You're a beacon of consistency but sometimes, you could afford to loosen up a little. Your grandchild won't be ruined by a bag of crisps or an extra story before bed now and then.

MOSTLY B: **BALANCED GRANNY**

You've got the right balance between Naughty Granny and Nice Granny. You respect the parents' decisions, but you're also aware that sometimes parents can go overboard on the rules and you see it as your role to challenge them – subtly – by allowing your grandchild a little extra freedom when they're around you. Don't go too far, and don't undermine the parents on anything serious, and you'll steer an excellent course between indulgence and good sense.

MOSTLY C: **REBEL GRANNY**

You're the original rock 'n' roll granny. Troublemaker, rule-breaker – you really don't think parental rules apply to your relationship with your grandchild, and are happy to ride roughshod over them. But while that can work when they're too little to tell tales, what's going to happen when your grandchild can talk and reports you to their mum and dad? You're risking a real showdown with your family, so try and steer a little more within the lines. A bit of rule-breaking is fine but total disregard isn't ideal for anyone.

I don't always agree with the rules but I do try to make sure I stick to them. My daughter is pretty laid back, but she minds about things like organic vegetables, and free-range meat, whereas I'm not too fussy. She was brought up in the eighties, when it was all ready meals and frozen pizza, and she's perfectly OK. But because it matters so much to her, I try to go the extra mile though sometimes, I have to admit, I don't buy everything organic. As for bedtime, I have a rough rule that if my granddaughter is in bed by seven-thirty, I don't mind if she wants a story or to play a little game. I think grans tend to bend the rules a bit, and ultimately, it doesn't do any great harm.

Terri Harper, 63

CHAPTER 7

GRANNY'S BASIC
CHILD CARE
REFRESHER COURSE

6 I'd honestly forgotten everything I knew – I was
terrified, it was as though I'd never met a baby before. 9
Annette Parkinson, 73

It may all miraculously come back to you, like falling off
a log, riding a bike and taking candy from a baby (which
is only OK if you're hungry). Then again, if it's been a
good 30 years or more since you last changed a nappy
or pretended to be an unprivatized train chugging food
towards a reluctant baby's mouth, it might be helpful to
have a little basic refresher course.

Naturally, new parents are terrified when they first find
themselves alone with the baby – it's like having a live Ming
vase in the house, which is liable to tip itself over of its own
accord. And it may feel the same for you, unless you're a rather
young granny, in which case, you may recall everything with

terrible clarity, including what can happen when you don't get a nappy onto a boy baby in time. (Wee. In the eye.)

To see which skills you need to brush up, here's a quick quiz. Find out whether you're a pro or a panicker when it comes to baby care.

BABY-CARE QUIZ

1 Your grandchild is sobbing, she's had her tea, and there's still an hour until bedtime. Is it because:

a. She's tired and needs to be soothed

b. She didn't eat enough and is starving

c. She's ill and you should take her to a doctor

2 It's bathtime. Are you running the water:

a. Cold then hot, about 12 cm deep

b. Hot then cold, about 25 cm deep

c. You'd rather use the shower

3 Your grandchild is being weaned onto solids. Do you feed him:

a. Tiny bits of pureed fruit and veg, and baby porridge

b. Bits of anything he seems to like the look of, cut up small

c. Scrambled eggs, cheese cubes, cut-up fish fingers

4 **Your grandchild will not sleep when she's put down in the cot. Should you:**

a. Stick to the routine: check she's not hungry, put her back down, tiptoe out

b. Pick her up if she's really crying, and rock her back to sleep

c. Take her onto the sofa with you, or into your bed for warmth and comfort

5 **It's time to change his nappy. Are you:**

a. Lying him on his back, taking off the old one, cleaning front to back with baby wipes, and applying nappy cream

b. Holding him on your knee, sliding the new one on as you take the old one off, and washing him with soap and water

c. Unfolding a cloth nappy, because they're so much better for him than disposables

MOSTLY A: **EXPERT GRAN**

You are the modern pro of grannies, as up to speed as any childcare professional. It's likely you've had recent dealings with babies, know exactly what to do, and are fully aware of the most up-to-date thinking on child care. You can occasionally afford to be a little flexible but not when it comes to safety, such as bathing and appropriate foods. Go, Granny! Your grandchild is more than safe in your hands.

MOSTLY B: **GOOD ENOUGH GRAN**

Not bad, and you certainly remember a few things, the only trouble is a little of your knowledge may be outdated. Certain foods are not considered safe for weaning, such as salty foods, dairy, soy and nuts, as they can be both a choking hazard and an allergy trigger in young babies. You may be making a rod for your own back by picking the baby up when she won't sleep, and if she's crying the chances are high that if she's had a decent feed, she's tired. But it will all come back to you within a few weeks. In the meantime, relax and carry on doing your best.

MOSTLY C: **BACK TO BASICS GRAN**

It's been a while since you looked after babies, so even though undoubtedly well-intentioned, some of your methods are a little rusty. Small babies should not be given certain foods, including fish, dairy and eggs, and they definitely should not be soothed to sleep on the sofa, or in your bed, where you could fall asleep yourself and squash them.

Cloth nappies are popular with the eco-friendly parent, but an enormous hassle, so only use them if you're more worried about the planet than your grandchild's bottom, and bathwise, cold then hot, about 12 cm deep, is always the safest option for young babies. You will get there but a few reminders may be very useful before your first evening's babysitting.

THE BASICS

Crying

That wretched, sheet-tearing screaming is designed not only to drive you to extremes of guilty despair, but to get a baby's needs met when it can't yet say, 'Look here, I'm bloody starving, and you're not solving the problem.'

So there's usually no cause to panic – crying will not break a baby, it's supposed to do it. The exception is if the crying is accompanied by convulsions, fever, swelling, rigidity, sweating, or excessive diarrhoea and vomiting. In which case, head for the hospital. Otherwise, it's probably down to one of the following:

HUNGER: tiny babies have tiny stomachs, but that doesn't stop them being hungry. Sometimes breastfed babies struggle to get enough milk and supplementing with a bottle may be necessary.

CRYING TYPE: howling, building in intensity, clenched fists, moving their head looking for food.

TIREDNESS: if a baby feels tense, ill, or overstimulated, they may struggle to go to sleep but they're still exhausted.

CRYING TYPE: consistent, whingy, angry.

JUST FEELS LIKE CRYING: this is normal, especially in very young babies around two months, and it can go on for hours, which is distressing, but not life-threatening.

CRYING TYPE: relentless, comes on suddenly, bawling, shuddering breaths.

ILLNESS: colic, which causes pain in the tummy, or teething, will cause a baby to cry, as will a fever of any kind.

CRYING TYPE: weak, mewling, piteous, building to a crescendo if it isn't cured. If they're in pain, it's likely the back will arch, and they'll grunt and clench their fists, or bring their legs in, which could signal stomach pain.

If it's accompanied by any other symptoms, or you suspect a fever, take him to a doctor as soon as possible.

I was very out of practice, and when I babysat for my son's newborn twins, the crying floored me. One would start, and set the other off – plus it was hard to tell whether, just because one was hungry or tired, the other was too, or whether they were just joining in. I found that dummies helped a lot, though I know some people disapprove, and I ended up playing them classical music – that really helped; Mozart was particularly good at calming them down. My best advice is not to panic – run through the checklist (pain, tiredness, hunger) and if it's just crying for the sake of crying, stay calm and soothing. If you need a break, leave the room, rather than lose your temper through stress.

Nella Hughes, 59

Sleeping

Many, many babies won't sleep. It does not automatically mean there's anything wrong, they may just like being awake. In fact 25 per cent of under-fives have sleep 'issues'. Your grandchild may wake in the night, or take hours to fall asleep, and because they'll be tired, they'll probably be crying, too.

This will take a major toll on the parents, so if you've stepped in to give them a break, here's what you should know about babies who won't sleep.

❋ Try not to rock him to sleep when he's newborn: or he may struggle to get to sleep without being rocked for hours. Put him on his back, and sit nearby, until he falls asleep. If this leads to violent crying or if he can't sleep without cuddling, try lying him down and stroking his head. If he's very distressed pick him up, cuddle him, and then put him down again. It will help if the parents also do this. You may simply have to rock him to sleep for a while but rest assured, no 15-year-old needs his gran to rock him to sleep, so it will change in time.

❋ Give him a reassuring object from home: a teddy, blanket or mobile (hanging, not the phone kind). If he's at your house, having familiar objects nearby will help.

❋ Keep up the home routine, whether that's bath, story, bed, or cuddle, bed, musical mobile; knowing that things will happen in a set order is reassuring, and more likely to help him fall asleep feeling secure.

✳ Baby massage: which is really just stroking, and *very gently* rubbing your thumbs in little circles on his back, front, legs and arms. This can help a baby to relax, and will encourage bonding and promote sleep, but check with his parents if they're happy for you to massage him. If he's not used to it, begin with just his legs, to see if he enjoys it. And make sure his last feed is digested before you start . . .

✳ Controlled crying: it's unlikely you'll be doing this, as his gran. The problem comes if his parents are advocates of 'controlled crying', which means from about six months, settling him to sleep, letting him cry for a bit before settling again with minimum fuss and leaving the room. The idea is that eventually, he will learn to sleep within a short period of time. If you don't agree with the method, but the parents do, unfortunately, you really need to go along with it, or you'll undo all their work by picking him up and rocking him. If you really hate the idea; just tell them you'd rather not babysit until the method has worked.

Feeding

Many parents get themselves into a huge state over feeding. They assume their baby will starve to death if she doesn't absorb at least some butternut squash puree, and that a rejection of mashed strawberry and banana is a rejection of themselves and their love. Well, it isn't, some babies are just fussier eaters than others, and when they're hungry they will eat. If they're really not eating anything, a health professional will advise, but let's assume that when you're on duty, your grandchild is not ill. Here's what you need to know . . .

Newborn

Bottles of formula or breast milk are all that's required. If you don't have a sterilizer, every time you make a new bottle, wash the bottle and its component parts in hot soapy water and boil for ten minutes with sterilizing solution. This is obviously better done straight after a feed than just before the next one, when she's puce with rage and hunger. Use cooled boiled water to make up the formula (it is very easy, the packet tells you how many scoops) and shake the bottle – with cap on, unless you want to redecorate your kitchen with hot milk spray. Test the temperature on your wrist – if it's too hot, stand it in a pan of cold water. Every baby's different, but the rough rule is between 50–200 ml of formula per kilogram of her body weight per day. Or just feed when she's hungry and she'll stop when she's had enough. If the baby seems to have trouble getting the milk out, check the teat isn't blocked. When it comes to heating bottles, don't use a microwave (as it can heat unevenly) – warm it in a pan of hot water instead.

Weaning

The current advice is no earlier than six months but when a large baby is starving at four or five months, it's a bold parent who won't give in and offer a few rusks. But it's a controversial area, so try to follow the parents' lead on this. Good foods to try with six-month-olds are: baby porridge or baby rice; pureed fruits like mango or apple; mashed veg like carrot or sweet potato. There's every chance she'll spit it back in your face, but it can take between eight and 15 tries before a baby will take to a new taste, so keep a damp cloth handy, and try again later.

7–9 months

Introduce more foods, like pasta, potatoes, meat, fish and cheese. Some may not agree with her, so only offer little amounts at first.

Some babies will prefer to pick food up with their hands, and although a Jackson Pollock made from carrot may not be an ideal scenario, if it's the only way she'll eat, you may as well go with it but perhaps invest in an apron. This is why grannies in the olden days wore housecoats.

9–12 months

She's cruising on the home strait towards actual meals now – even if they are chopped into cubes and served in a Hello Kitty dish. Be very careful of choking hazards like grapes, raisins or meat chopped too big – her teeth are the chopping equivalent of a blunt butter knife – but it's worth testing out various different foods. Follow the parents' lead though.

FOODS TO AVOID

- **PROCESSED FOODS:** they're often packed with salt, sugar and additives, so not good for babies. The exceptions are decent organic ready meals, specially designed for babies.

- **SALT:** too much is dangerous and it's not necessary to add any. Babies should have less than a gram of salt a day, and don't forget it's found in cheese, sausages and tinned foods like baked beans. Buy low-sugar and low-salt versions.

- **HONEY:** can contain bacteria that may cause 'infant botulism' – and you don't want to be the grandparent responsible for that hospital dash . . .

- **NUTS:** for obvious, choke-based and possible allergy reasons.

- **LOW-FAT OR PROTEIN-PACKED FOOD:** this is not made for small stomachs to process – keep food as natural as possible.

- **SUGAR:** bad for teeth and bad for blood sugar – natural sugars in fruit are better. But if her parents allow biscuits or cakes, a few bites won't do great harm, just don't ever rely on sweet food as ways to keep a baby quiet. Two words: Augustus Gloop.

GETTING FOOD INTO YOUR GRANDCHILD

You need a highchair. Really you do. Improvising by holding her on your lap is a fast track to finding yourself plastered with banana, trying to restrain a human eel while spat-out food crop-sprays the sofa. Very small babies can of course be bottle fed in your lap but any solid food requires a plastic tray, spoon, bowl, and straps to hold her in.

Use a small plastic baby spoon, and leave plenty of time – trying to rush a baby's mealtime is like trying to turn a tanker round in thirty seconds. It will not happen. If she won't eat after several attempts, give up and come back to it later.

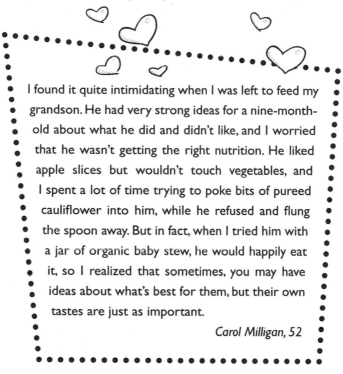

I found it quite intimidating when I was left to feed my grandson. He had very strong ideas for a nine-month-old about what he did and didn't like, and I worried that he wasn't getting the right nutrition. He liked apple slices but wouldn't touch vegetables, and I spent a lot of time trying to poke bits of pureed cauliflower into him, while he refused and flung the spoon away. But in fact, when I tried him with a jar of organic baby stew, he would happily eat it, so I realized that sometimes, you may have ideas about what's best for them, but their own tastes are just as important.

Carol Milligan, 52

If she'll only eat one type of food, don't sweat it, nobody reaches the age of 18, turns up to college, and says, 'I'm afraid I can only eat carrot sticks and hummus. Sorry.' So just let her be.

THINGS YOU NEED TO FEED A BABY:

- Highchair
- Small plastic spoon
- Plastic bowl
- Wet wipes or damp cloth
- A bib for the baby
- An apron for you

BATHS

Baths can be terrifying with newborn babies. They feel as slippery as an oil-coated bowling ball, and as fragile as an ancient scroll. You think you'll drop them, drown them, bash their head on the taps, make the water too cold, too hot . . . but it's quite simple.

If they're very young, get a plastic baby bath, fill it about 10 cm deep with cold, then hot water, to avoid scalding, test the temperature (traditionally with your elbow, but really, your hand is perfectly fine), then lower your grandchild in, bottom first, supporting their head and back as you go. A bit of splashing, then lift them out onto a towel that's already in your lap, and swaddle them in it.

If they're bigger and you're using the real bath, don't run the water more than 12 cm deep, and never ever leave the child alone in the bath – even for seconds, even if he can sit up alone, even if you're just running to the airing cupboard to get a clean towel – just don't.

The bath is the area, however, where older grans, or those with bad backs may struggle to lift without jerking, so if there's nobody to help, and you're worried, don't offer to bath the baby. You can top and tail him – face, creases (neck, under the arms), and round the bum and front – with cotton wool dipped in warm water, and pat him dry. Or go truly old-school, and bath him in the sink.

NAPPIES

Let's assume you're tasked with using disposables – because if you're being asked to use cloth by your son or daughter, you'll do a lot better watching a YouTube video of how to put one on than you will from reading a convoluted explanation. So google away.

THINGS YOU NEED TO CHANGE A BABY:

- Changing mat
- Nappies suitable for size
- Wet wipes or warm water and cotton wool
- Nappy cream
- Wrestling skills

Disposables need to be changed whenever they're wet or full. For the former, you can check with a quick sniff or test with your finger. For the latter, the time-honoured 'lift and sniff' manoeuvre remains the easiest way, and if you don't need to get close to tell, then it's probably long overdue.

HOW TO CHANGE A NAPPY

* Lay your grandchild on a changing mat – on the floor is best, if your knees can take it, to prevent him rolling off as you reach for nappy cream.

* Undo his poppers, whisk off his jogging bottoms, unfurl her tutu, and make sure there's no cloth in the way where stray poo could find itself.

* Take off the dirty nappy and bag it, while holding the baby's legs up slightly to avoid any poo travelling elsewhere. Get your cotton wool or wet wipe, and swish from front to back, cleaning their bottom thoroughly. Wipe round and under the front area.

* Take your (already opened) fresh nappy, and lay it under their bum, before adding a thin layer of a nappy cream if necessary.

* Do up the nappy using the tabs, and then attempt to get a knitted octopus into an inner tube. Or at least, trying to stuff a baby back into the bottom half of a Babygro can feel like that. Sometimes, it might be easier to re-dress them altogether.

* Dispose of nappy, wash hands, lift clean baby. Done.

POTTY TRAINING

This is up to the parents so no little asides like 'I thought he'd be dry at night by now'. A popular method nowadays is to let the toddler roam nappyless so he can hopefully go to the potty when it's time to wee or poo, but it can be high risk if you value your rugs, so have the discussion before they embark on this method. Otherwise, follow their lead – if they plonk him on the potty every hour or so, do the same – and never, ever get cross if he doesn't quite make it. If it's too soon, you'll soon find out because he won't use the potty.

PUSHCHAIRS, PLAYPENS, AND SAFETY EQUIPMENT

Pram

The golden days of the Silver Cross carriage pram are fading (unless you're a royal baby), and most prams now are collapsible to fit easily in the boot of the car. Ask the parents for a full lesson, write it all down in a notebook if you need to but do not go out without a full knowledge of exactly which lever and which strap is required to put it up or down.

The first time I took Betsy out on my own, I realized, just before we got on the bus, that I had no idea how to collapse the pushchair. I was holding her in one arm, struggling to find the lever and find the right bit to pull with the other and there was an impatient queue behind me. It was mortifying. Luckily, a kind dad came to my rescue but then I had to unfold it at the other end, which took me ten minutes to work out. If your daughter says, 'It's really simple,' don't believe her. It isn't, and I'd advise any fellow gran to practise, a lot, before they venture outside.

Lynne Keller, 60

Car seat

Safety is paramount in the car. Again, insist on a lesson, watch the manufacturer's video, practise and do not put him in it and pull away from the kerb until you're 100 per cent certain that you've installed it absolutely right. If someone has forgotten the car seat, and it's only a short trip, and he could sit on your knee – **don't go**. If something goes wrong, you will never, ever forgive yourself.

Highchair

Should be simple enough but always make sure the straps are fitted properly on the baby because they have a staggering knack of wriggling out of the shoulder straps. And be wary of booster seats that screw onto the table as they have been known to fall off.

Baby bouncer

Most fit over the door frame. They can be a godsend if you're busy in the kitchen – but always triple-check it's properly fixed. Alternatively, you can get a very comfy seat bouncer.

Playpen

If you're using a playpen make sure the sides are properly extended, so it doesn't suddenly collapse with your bewildered grandchild in the middle.

Stair gate

These can be tricky to fit and if the part that fixes it against the stairs is loose, then disaster can ensue. Again, if you're not confident, get someone who's done it before to set it up and learn how to use it so you're not reduced to climbing over it and locking your back, because you don't understand the catch.

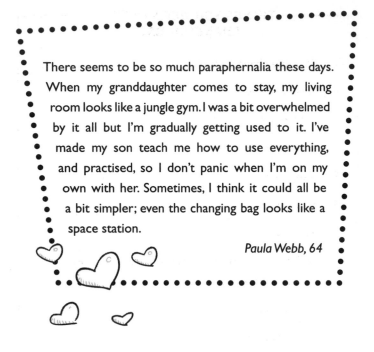

There seems to be so much paraphernalia these days. When my granddaughter comes to stay, my living room looks like a jungle gym. I was a bit overwhelmed by it all but I'm gradually getting used to it. I've made my son teach me how to use everything, and practised, so I don't panic when I'm on my own with her. Sometimes, I think it could all be a bit simpler; even the changing bag looks like a space station.

Paula Webb, 64

THE CHANGING BAG

This is the red box of baby care – the vital container of all things baby-related, and when it's left with you, guard it carefully.

THINGS YOU NEED IN THE CHANGING BAG

- Portable changing mat

- Muslin cloths

- Wet wipes

- Change of baby clothes

- Nappies

- Nappy bags

- Nappy cream

- Bottle (and formula if you're going out for a while)/ or a jar of food and a spoon

- Drinking cup

- Toys/a baby book

You'll probably collect other bits and bobs along the way but try not to get too weighed down. A change of nappy, emergency spare clothes, food or bottle and a drink should do it unless you're trekking in the Andes.

CHAPTER 8

ADVANCED MODERN CHILD CARE

❝ I don't know how I lived without Skype. It's a godsend now my family are far away. ❞

Lilly Williams, 66

With your own grandma, you probably had a whole range of options for keeping in touch. That came down to visits, letters or phone calls (but only after 6 p.m.) Your own mum, if she was around for your children's teen years, might have embraced email. But for you, the possibilities for keeping in touch with grandchildren are almost intimidatingly varied and if you don't live close by, it really pays to understand what the options are. Of course, by the time you've had this book for a while, there's every chance communication will be extended to personal satellites that can be activated by thought waves. But until then, you can maximize your time with them, even if you can't be there in person. Then there's baby-listening devices, mobiles, sending and receiving pictures and videos . . . so here's what you need to know to thoroughly embrace the modern world.

HOW TO KEEP IN TOUCH

Unless they live in the next village, street or a short drive away, one of your biggest concerns will be maintaining an ongoing relationship with your grandchildren as they get older, and if they're still little, being able to see pictures, videos and even wave and chat to them online.

FACEBOOK

This is the big daddy of all the social media sites, and most people I know are on it. You can chat privately online with your daughter or son, they can send you pictures, and you can also post pictures and videos and share news on your own page.

PROS: It allows words, photos and video, it's instant, you can have privacy settings that mean only your family and friends can see your posts, and you can get a phone app that means you can instantly upload photos and videos, and see pictures of your grandchildren.

CONS: The privacy settings sometimes change, which can be confusing, and you can't video chat on Facebook. You may not want to be sent friend requests from people you may or may not know.

TWITTER

Also huge, Twitter is where many people get their information nowadays. Set up an account (very easy) and you can Tweet about anything you like and contact other Twitter users directly. You can also attach photos and videos to your Tweets, and see other people's. If you have a large family, you can set up a hashtag such as #williamsfamily so everyone's Tweets can be seen in one place, and you can also direct message in private.

PROS: It's fast, fun and allows quick bursts of information to be exchanged. Younger people are very at ease with it, and it's less personal and time-consuming than Facebook.

CONS: Everything you say must be reduced to 140 characters or less, it's not usually used as a 'private' app, so followers can see what you say, and it's not particularly child-friendly for pre-teens.

WHATSAPP/WECHAT

Very popular in certain countries, this is a virtually free text messaging service, so you can text your daughter's Android phone in Australia from your iPhone in London and it will cost almost nothing. It sends messages over WiFi when available, hence it's virtually free to use. Very useful across all platforms for exchanging messages and sending photos. As of 2014, people around the world were sharing more than 700 million photos and 100 million videos on WhatsApp daily.

PROS: Free, fast and it doesn't matter what Smartphone you have. Great for texting family who live abroad.

CONS: No phone calls, and everyone has to sign up to the app. No good if your grandchildren are too small to text.

SNAPCHAT

Loved by teenagers, Snapchat lets you take a photo, write or draw on it, and send it to a contact (or all of them) also on Snapchat, then it disappears within seconds. Older children tend to like the funny possibilities of drawing on faces, teens like the fact that embarrassing pics vanish. But it's more for fun than a regular way of staying in touch.

PROS: It's fun, and a good way to engage with a pre-teen or teen who might not be around much for chatting.

CONS: Pictures vanish (unless you take a screenshot), and it only allows very short written messages.

VIBER

A free phone app, which allows you to make phone calls, and also offers a messaging service with jolly stickers to illustrate the conversation. It only works via WiFi or 3G, and the other user has to have the Viber app installed. It's very useful if you like talking on the phone and your family lives abroad.

PROS: You don't need to register, it's easy to download, and it's free.

CONS: It doesn't work on older phone models, and the other user has to have the Viber app.

SKYPE

Free video calls, works on Smartphone or computers, and allows you to chat with people anywhere in the world. You can even have multiple calls with more than one number at once. It's an immediate way of seeing and hearing your family at the same time and they can see and hear you. Also can be used as a voice-only call.

I live over 100 miles from my family. Skype is brilliant for me – the grandchildren are only three and five so too little to write, but they will sit in front of the computer and chat away because it's something they're growing up with and they are completely at ease with it. I found it rather odd at first, and it made me miss them more, but now I find it's a brilliant way to 'top up' our time together, make sure they know exactly who Grandma and Grandad are, and if they're a bit sleepy, we might even sing a song over Skype, or tell them a bedtime story. It's not a substitute for real time together, but it definitely helps.

Sue Wessel, 54

PROS: The next best thing to being in the same room – live streaming so you can chat and see your grandkids at the same time – and costs nothing.

CONS: The picture can be very pixelated and there can be a delay, depending on connection, it occasionally fails, and you have to be in front of your phone or computer.

EMAIL

Old-school (well, it is now). You have an email address, you write online messages, letters, and so forth to their email address and you can attach pictures, though big files may be difficult to send. Good if you enjoy letter writing as it allows time to express yourself properly, send detailed information and exchange news at length and you can keep the messages.

PROS: Good for older children and teenagers to catch up with you if you're not on Facebook, and it lets you write as much as you like.

CONS: Less personal, visuals are harder to send, rather old-fashioned for teenagers to use.

BABY GADGETS – WHICH ONES ARE WORTH HAVING?

But while mobile and computer apps are all very well if you live miles away, how can you embrace the modern world if you live round the corner? Well, if you're willing to get up to speed, there are several gadgets and apps that can make your grandmothering life a whole lot easier, from microwave steam sterilizers to iPhone baby-listening apps.

A vaguely Luddite fear that somehow technology is cheating is perfectly understandable – remember the shock a few years ago, when that video of a baby trying to 'swipe' the pages of a magazine went viral? (Well, perhaps you don't, because you're still not quite at the YouTubing-funny-baby-videos level of techno-awareness, but rest assured, the days when that kind of thing was shocking are gone, and many babies are now swiping and pressing the iPad screen long before their first birthday, happily assuming that something will pop up and play a tune in response to their fat fingers.)

And you may as well accept it because while picture books and soft toys still have a significant place in the modern baby's life, they are growing up in an age of technology that previously wasn't dreamed of, and if you want to understand their world, you're a lot better off joining in. Download a few apps to amuse them, and you may find yourself deeply grateful to have access to plinky classical tunes accompanied by swirly visuals the next time you're desperate to get her to sleep; or you may find that being able to press a button that makes the requisite farmyard noises along with the pictures is an improvement on your own attempts at being a chicken.

The list of communications apps is endless – there's sign language apps, apps featuring favourite characters, apps that sing, play tunes, talk, squeak . . . If you're a little rusty technologically, press-gang someone youthful to show you how to search and download apps – then there'll be no stopping you.

I was very anti-technology at first. I could just about cope with a steam sterilizer, but anything online wasn't for me. But when Lucia was born, her mum and dad loved the fact that they could use their iPhones as a baby-listening device, or play her music and games when they were travelling. Now she's three and watches Disney films on the iPad, and I have to say, I have caught up a bit. I love snuggling up in bed with her in the morning and watching films. I honestly don't think there's anything wrong with embracing the modern world, as long as you don't treat it as a virtual babysitter.

Joan Pearson, 56

Of course, you may decide that the world of fast broadband connection, online communications, baby-listening apps and iPad swiping is not for you. In which case, stock up on library books, make phone calls, write letters – that's perfectly fine. But while technology may carry certain risks, such as encouraging laziness, security issues, built-in obsolescence, it can also be a hugely helpful learning tool, a supportive back-up when you're tired or busy, and a way to stay in touch across the miles. So don't knock it until you've tried it.

CHAPTER 9

WHAT IF THEY BREAK UP?

❝ I had sleepless nights when my son split with his partner – not only was I worried about him, I was also terrified I'd never see my grandsons again. ❞

Barbara McAdam, 67

It's unlikely – but possible – they've split up before your grandchild has even been born. But more usually, the pressure of young children tends to exacerbate any existing relationship problems and sometimes they can push it over the edge into a break-up. Unless you actively hate your son- or daughter-in-law, this will be a huge sadness for you, and on top of that, you may either be called upon to offer enormous amounts of support, or conversely, fear that your access to the grandchildren will be a problem, particularly if you're the paternal grandma, and they are living primarily with their mum. And it's true, unfortunately, that when a couple splits up, initially at least, there may be less time to visit during parental access visits and weekends because their dad will want to spend one-to-one time with them. But it's also vital to keep the

My son had an affair and split from his wife when the children were two and five. They'd always had problems, but I'd hoped having a family would help. And of course, he behaved like a prat but I knew he was unhappy, and my primary concern was for my grandchildren. He had generous access and saw them two nights a week and one weekend night, so I suggested that they come for tea here on Thursdays, so they could have some family time with their dad away from his rather bleak new flat. It worked really well – my husband and I are closer to the children than ever, and now everything's settled down, we often see them at weekends too, and my ex daughter-in-law will ask me to babysit when she goes out. It was traumatic and very upsetting but I'm so glad I maintained the relationship I have with the children.

Louise Pearson, 62

consistency and security of a family unit going – and that's where you come in.

You will almost certainly know if things are wrong between your grandchildren's parents. But keeping quiet until asked is, again, a very useful skill at this point. Saying 'You seem really tetchy with each other, is something wrong?' won't help, though a gentle 'Is everything OK between you?' might lead to an outpouring. If you're asked your opinion on whether your son or daughter should stay or go, don't automatically assume that it's better for the children if they stay. Living in a home full of tension is not always better, and two happy, separated parents can be a vast improvement on together, unhappy ones, particularly if the child is very young when it happens.

Once a split is agreed – or spontaneously happens – you'll be both concerned for your child and almost certainly wondering what will happen to your relationship with your grandchild. Ideally, the answer is 'nothing' – you'll be recognized as family, and see them as much as ever, even if the circumstances have altered. But in the worst case scenario, the primary caring parent can move away and take the kids with her, or refuse to let them see you at all. This is hugely stressful situation for everyone involved, and if it does come to that, there are several things you should not do.

WHAT NOT TO SAY

✳   'But what about the children?' Is not helpful. They are parents, they have already thought of this.

✳   'But what about me? Will I still see the children?' This is not their primary concern, mid break-up. Be supportive without being demanding.

✳   'The children could come and live with us.' Not in a million years, unless the parents are provenly inadequate, abusive, or dead. Don't even think about it.

✳   'Your father and I haven't always been happy but we stuck it out for your sake.' Do you truly think your child will turn around and say, 'Good point! Oh well, in that case we're back together.' No, they won't. So don't say it.

✳   'I never liked him.' Your daughter once did and he is the father of her child, with whom she will need to have a good working relationship for many years to come. It will be best if you do, too.

✳   'Well, she needn't expect me to babysit while she's gallivanting.' Really? Because ultimately, it's about what's best for the children, not whether you approve of your daughter-in-law's social life. Try and keep that in mind.

There are, however, certain things you can say which might actually be helpful. Try:

✳   'What practical help do you need at the moment?' Saying, 'I'm here for you' is vague and people don't always like to ask – demanding specifics is a good way to find out what's really needed.

✳   'Would you like me to have him for a few days while the dust settles?' It's helpful and sensible, if things are fraught, to offer overnight babysitting but bear in mind that young children will need to know where their mum and dad are and when they will see them again.

✳   'You did your best, and the children will be fine.' Yes it's a cliché but no less valid. Every parent in a break-up feels guilty and anything you can say to help will be appreciated.

✳ 'Let's draw up a plan – if you're on your own, would
   you like me to have him one or two days a week?' Or
   whatever you can manage – being a single parent is
   very hard, and all help should be appreciated.

But what if the finances are in chaos, your daughter or
son has been left holding the baby, and it looks like they're
moving in with you? Deep breath . . . here's how to make
it manageable.

IF THEY'RE MOVING IN

There is a huge difference between providing part-time
support as a granny, and being on call full-time. It's a bit
like sleeping in the factory, when the relentless, dictatorial
boss is sleeping in the adjacent office, and could wake up
any moment and demand you get back on the production
line, and nobody cares if it's 3 a.m.

That's why it's essential to agree the rules in advance.
Admittedly, your son or daughter may be traumatized,
grief-stricken, and in need of huge amounts of support and
meanwhile, the children aren't going to bath themselves.
It's a natural instinct to throw your arms round them all
and cry, 'Stay as long as you want!'

But it's also not that simple. Because despite your
unconditional love for your family, there are certain areas
you need to discuss in order to make sure your living
together doesn't end in rows and resentment.

ESSENTIAL QUESTIONS TO ASK

◆ How long is it likely to be for?

◆ Is there a suitable room for the baby/children and all their things?

◆ Will you all eat together or cook and eat separately? If so, who goes first, and what's the washing-up policy?

◆ Will there be a financial contribution to bills and food or are you going to keep paying for household bills?

◆ How much childcare will you be expected to do and, at least roughly, on which days?

◆ Bathroom usage: when do the children have their bath, what time in the morning does everyone shower?

◆ TV: will you want to watch TV at the same time, or opt for a timeshare view?

◆ Housework: who does what? Who cleans up after the children and cooks their meals?

◆ What's the policy on their dad (or mum) coming to visit them at your home?

◆ If there's a new partner on the scene are they welcome to visit or stay the night?

Everyone's answers to these questions will be different but if you don't ask them before the suitcases arrive, you could be heading for trouble.

I'd just taken early retirement from teaching and I was looking forward to some peace and quiet, when my daughter told us she was splitting up with her husband. He left her with two under-fives, and the only option was for them to sell the family home, which meant she'd be stuck in a small rented flat, and forking out for childcare as she lived 20 miles away from us. It seemed sensible to offer that she should bring the kids and come back home, at least temporarily. She was grateful but I know she felt she had no choice. We should have sat down immediately and agreed the rules. But because it happened quickly, it ended up being quite chaotic. She'd suddenly ask me to look after them, or she'd be on the phone arguing with her ex and I'd end up doing bed and bath time – it was exhausting. They stayed for a year, and it was lovely having the children, but I was relieved when they moved out. I wish we'd discussed it properly, and agreed a strategy beforehand.

Julia Simons, 58

That's the problem with opening up your home and heart as a gran: you are never going to be the primary concern. Of course, your feelings should be taken into account and your views respected but the likelihood is that whether your child meets someone else and moves in, gets back with their ex, or goes it alone, it's only ever going to be a temporary arrangement, so try to maintain the interests and hobbies you enjoyed before the family boomeranged back or you may struggle to adjust.

WHAT IF YOU CAN'T SEE YOUR GRANDCHILDREN?

There's one big problem with the parents splitting up – if it's acrimonious, you have very few rights regarding your grandchildren. You can love them like a mother, care for them regularly, devote your life savings to buying them ponies and bicycles, but if their primary carer decides you're not going to see them any more, you may well have a long and fraught battle on your hands. At the time of writing, there is no law that permits grandparental access regardless of the parents' wishes unless the children are old enough to have their view taken into account (over 12, usually), or you can prove that their parent is unfit. But the chances are, if you're struggling to see them, so is your son and daughter, and a distraught parent is more likely to get their day in court than a devastated grandparent. British law says that only people who are parentally responsible for the children can apply for a contact order in court. You can, however, apply for 'Permission to apply for a contact order', and the family court will consider the circumstances, based on how much contact you normally have with your grandchild, and whether you having contact could potentially harm them in any way. If the court thinks it would be beneficial to the grandchildren to continue seeing you, you can apply for a contact order, but if a parent (or both of them) object then you may have to attend a full hearing, where evidence will be weighed. On that basis, you will need a lawyer – and it will not be cheap.

It will only go in your favour – and not necessarily even then – if the court truly agrees that the child's interests are best served by a continuing relationship, in the face of their parent's reluctance. Generally, unless there are clear problems, a court will aim to reunite children and grandparents, but there are no guarantees, and it is a long and arduous process that may end up causing more hostility and mean the children end up worrying about seeing you, or being treated as pawns in an adult conflict. If that's the likely outcome, it could be better – albeit painful – to step back and be a loving grandparent from a distance for a while.

If you do get a contact order, the access arrangements will be laid out, including face-to-face meetings, and even texting and video calls. It will generally spell out the terms on which you will see the children, whether they will spend the night or longer, or just an hour with you under the supervision of a parent, or even social worker. There is a problem, however, if the parent refuses to comply with the contact order – very few judges will imprison the children's primary carer, and the alternative is a fine, which they may not be able to pay, meaning that, effectively, their hands are tied.

You may, however, manage to get an 'indirect contact' order, which means emails, gifts and calls are permitted. This might be a better option, at least temporarily, if tensions between the parents – or you – are running very high.

My son and his partner had a very difficult break-up. She tried to stop the children seeing him so he spent three years in court, because they were not old enough to state their own feelings. It was terrible for him, and also for us. I tried to send cards and letters, but she threw them out. I couldn't get a contact order to see them, because my son wasn't able to get close to them, and his ex would not have let it happen, assuming he would see his children at our house. It was devastating, and it only ended when the youngest turned 12, and was able to say that she wanted to see her dad and us. It's still very difficult with their mum, and now we see them perhaps a couple of times a year. It's a great sadness, but at least we have some contact now and can send them presents and letters via our son.

Angela Dunne, 66

If you find yourself in this grim situation, all is not lost. Children get older, and things seldom stay the same. Try, if possible, not to become bitter, and never criticize their parents' actions to the children, however insane and hurtful they appear to be.

In the meantime, you can try:

* Contacting the Grandparents' Association for advice, support and information. They will try to help

grandparents who have lost contact with grandchildren due to family disputes and splits. They also support grandparents who are full-time carers for their grandchildren, and their educational needs. There's a general helpline, welfare benefits advice, support groups and fact sheets at www.grandparents-association.org.uk.

* Look online for legal contacts specializing in family breakdown, and other support services.
* Sending birthday and Christmas presents but don't ever refer to the dispute or how sad you are not to see them. Anything that smacks of emotional manipulation, however well meant, is unfair on the children.
* Making a phone call on the same day every week or month to keep up a sense of routine and consistency.
* Exchanging photos and chat online via Facebook, Skype or various apps like WhatsApp.

Of course, these only work if your grandchildren are old enough to communicate; if not, it may be a waiting game.

SUPPORTING A SINGLE PARENT

If the split is relatively amicable, and access is agreed, then it's time to make the best of it. It may well be a shock, and far from what you hoped (especially if you paid for the wedding), but divorce rates in many countries are high.

That means there's a good chance you might end up being the first port of call for your single-parent son or daughter, which could equate to plenty of time with the grandchildren but also exhaustion. Try to set boundaries: it's all right not to be available every single time they need to nip to the shops or go on a date. Encourage them to form friendships with other parents rather than solely relying on you because there's a good chance that they'll end up in a new relationship, and you don't want to feel supplanted by someone else in the children's lives.

I was constantly at my daughter's house when she was a single mum to her little girl, Edie. I'd look after her whenever Jenny needed me to; I'd make her tea, put her to bed – I was like Edie's second mum. Then Jenny met Ian, and he moved in. Suddenly I wasn't needed in the same way. I understood that they needed time together, and of course, Edie needed to get used to Ian, but I felt so redundant – I'd made being there for my family my main purpose, and I was relegated to part-time visitor. Now I realize that I shouldn't have allowed Jenny to rely on me quite so much, but she needed it at the time, and I'd probably do it again.

Lesley Walker, 66

THE NEW PARTNER

After a split, there's every chance that your child will meet a new partner. If so, he or she will undoubtedly have a relationship with your grandchild. So while your temptation might be to doubt, and to worry that the new relationship won't last, the best thing you can do is get to know them and offer support to them as a family. If you inherit step-grandchildren, this can be tricky because your natural instinct will almost certainly be to favour the 'biological' grandchildren. (This can also be an issue with your own step-children and their babies.) The only fair advice, however, is don't. Nobody can legislate for how much you love a child, but if you're buying pricy gifts for the 'real' grandchild, and fobbing off the others with cheap plastic, it will only serve to cause a rift between the children and their parents. Never show favouritism – even if you feel it.

And remember, statistically, the first year of a baby's life is often the catalyst for a split in unhappy couples. The added pressures, financially and emotionally – even the strain of post-natal depression – can push things to breaking point. It's sad but if it does happen, it's not the end of the world. Families come in all shapes and sizes, and it will be a huge help to your son or daughter, and the children, to know you're there for them.

CHAPTER 10

LONG-DISTANCE GRANDPARENTING

❝ We'd got used to living hundreds of miles away from our daughters, and looked forward to visits. But when they both got pregnant within a year of each other, we had a real dilemma – whether to stay, or move nearer to them. ❞

Susan Keyes, 68

The big dilemma of new grandparents everywhere is all down to location, location, location. Of course, if you've lived in the same village as your children all your life, and everyone pops round to each other's houses every five minutes, that's perfectly fine. What's not so good is when your children went to university, say, a few hundred miles away, got a job there, decided to stay, and are now about to have your first grandchild, and are in need of support. Of course, you want to be around for them but you also quite like your life the way it is, you love your house, and unless they move closer to you (which a lot of younger people do, once the reality of paying for childcare sinks in) you may be stuck between a rock and a hard place, either constantly shuttling up and down the country, sleeping on a futon that gives you a back like a pretzel, or else racked with guilt, wondering whether you should sell up and move to a one-bedroom flat because then you'll only be three stops away.

But before you do anything drastic, think through all the options and the pros and cons of each.

OPTION 1: ALL MOVE IN TOGETHER

When my daughter Karen found out she was pregnant, she'd just been made redundant, and her partner, Anthony, had taken a pay cut. We'd been thinking about downsizing and after a lot of discussion it made sense for us all to sell up and buy a place together. We had a lot of reservations, as to how much room we'd all have, and whether the baby would keep us awake all night, but we've been living together for six months now and it's wonderful to live with our grandson, and watch him grow. There are certain things we have to negotiate, like who cooks and when we use the bathroom, but for now, it's a perfect arrangement for all of us.

Kathleen Bennett, 66

PROS: You're on hand for childcare, and you have company in retirement (if you are retired). You'll get to spend plenty of time with your family, and watch your grandchild grow at close quarters. It's also a lot cheaper if you share the bills, mortgage or rent. If your child and their partner move into your home, it can give it a new lease of life, and ease the burden of household maintenance as you get older.

CONS: It may not work long term – unless you have a big house, you may find you're all on top on each other, and if another baby comes along, it may be too much of a squash, and mean you're back to square one, living separately. It can be difficult to divide chores and childcare, and it can have a negative impact on the relationship with your grown-up children if there are areas of tension. It can mean relocating to a new area.

A good idea if:

- You can find a place that's big enough, which everyone can afford

- You're happy to negotiate before you move in, over chores, childcare and kitchen/bathroom use

- You're ready for a change

- You get on very well with your grown-up child and their partner

- You're able to offer childcare when needed

- You've already discussed the big issues, starting with money, length of arrangement, and who gets which room

OPTION 2: MOVE NEARER BUT NOT TOO NEAR

My son lived in Manchester with his partner, because of work, while we were still living near London. But when they decided to start a family, I didn't like the idea that we were 200 miles away; I worried we wouldn't see the baby much plus Sarah's parents live abroad, so we felt they'd really struggle without family close by. We talked to them about it, and while we didn't really want to move to another city, we realized that if we lived 30 or 40 miles away, that made it much easier for us to get over there when they needed us, and for the baby to come and stay overnight. We sold up and bought a cottage in Derbyshire, and now we see them at least once a fortnight – that just wouldn't have happened if we'd stayed put.

Alex Peters, 53

PROS: You're fairly close, without breathing down anyone's neck, particularly if you've had a lot of space in your relationship over the last few years and got used to the distance. You're near if they need you, but have room to live your life if they don't. You're far away enough to make visits to Granny a fun and interesting treat.

CONS: You have to move house if they don't. You might want to see more of them than the distance allows. You're far enough to make driving over more expensive and a hassle. If you work, you'll need to find another job, or think about retiring – all big life changes.

A good idea if:

- You're keen to see more of your family, but don't want to be round every day

- You're in need of a life change

- You don't mind being on call in emergencies

- You can drive, or live near good public transport

OPTION 3: MOVE NEARBY OR THEY MOVE NEARER TO YOU

My daughter and her husband moved back to our village in Lincolnshire when Betty was three, and Allie was pregnant again. They wanted the same kind of upbringing for the kids that Allie had enjoyed, and though it was never an option for them to move in with us – they like their independence, and so do we – they found a place two streets away, and I'm so glad they're close by. I now see Allie and the children almost every day; she'll drop them off while she gets her shopping, or I'll pop round for a cup of tea. I missed them terribly when they lived in Nottingham, and I am so glad that we can be part of their lives again. Having said that, if they hadn't moved we would have considered it, though I think I'd have struggled to leave my home.

Barbara Page, 61

PROS: You have all the benefits of having them near, without the hassle of living together. You get to see your family regularly, and be a part of the grandchildren's life on a regular basis. You're part of the same community. You're on hand for childcare whenever they need it.

CONS: You may have to move house if they can't move nearer to you. You may not like your new area as much. You might find that you're not used to spending so much time together, and you may feel taken for granted as a babysitter.

A good idea if:

● You miss your family and love seeing them

● You're happy to babysit regularly

● Your job isn't an issue

● You're happy to move to a new area, if they can't move to you

OPTION 4: STAY WHERE YOU ARE

It's been 15 years since my son left for university. We've lived up north and he's lived down south since then, and since he married Tash, it's where all their friends live, and they have a real community. We love our area, too, and are very settled. So although it caused us a few sleepless nights when Tash told us she was pregnant, we decided to stay where we are. Her parents and sister live quite near to them, so they have some support, and we plan visits in advance, so we can make the most of our time together. I do miss my granddaughter, but she'll be at school in a few years, and we'd be twiddling our thumbs in an area where we don't know anyone.

Mina Singer-Holmes, 59

PROS: You get to stay in your home. You can see your family when it's mutually convenient. Every visit is a treat and feels special. You can have your family to stay and enjoy seeing them properly with no distractions when they visit.

CONS: They're far away. You may feel left out if the other grandparents live close by. You may feel guilty that you're not able to help out enough. You might miss them.

A good idea if:

- You're used to living away from them

- You have a busy life already, and not much time to offer lots of babysitting

- You'd rather see them in short bursts

- You're happy to keep a little distance and independence for the foreseeable future

OPTION 5: EXTENDED VISITS

> My stepdaughter and her partner live in France. We don't want to move for many reasons, but we do have the pleasure of extended visits, for a week or two, three or four times a year. It's lovely to spend time with them at their home, and be part of our grandchildren's lives, plus when we're there, it means we don't have any distractions – I don't have to say 'Granny's busy,' because I have all the time in the world when we stay with them.
>
> *Annette Parkinson, 73*

PROS: When you're with them, there are no distractions. You can be part of daily life because you're all staying under the same roof. You have plenty of independence and time to live your own life when you're not seeing them. If they live abroad, you get the holiday as well as the family time.

CONS: It can be expensive to arrange visits. It might not always be convenient. You may find it difficult to drop in and out of your grandchildren's lives. You might find you miss them in between times. You may not like the 'house rules' of your adult child's home, and find it hard to adapt.

A good idea if:

 They live abroad, and for you, moving would be a huge upheaval

 You have fairly similar lifestyles, so getting used to their way of life isn't too difficult

 You enjoy being a 'treat' for the grandchildren, rather than an everyday fixture

 You're willing to devote your time to them when you visit (or they visit you)

Whatever you choose to do, bear in mind that while around 50 per cent of grandparents offer some childcare help, there's still an awful lot who don't, and living a long way away doesn't make you any less of a grandparent. Visits to grandparents can create some of childhood's happiest memories, the time together is all the more special, and you can create your own traditions that they associate with your house, whether that's baking, blackberry picking, or watching TV with a box of chocolates.

If you do move closer (or they move nearer to you, or in with you) be prepared for an occasionally rocky road. It's not always easy to accommodate your needs to those of your adult children, so remember that negotiation might be needed, in more areas than you'd think, and discuss anything that might be contentious before you sign the joint mortgage.

THE BEST OF ALL WORLDS

There is one simple solution to the how-close-is-too-close conundrum. And that's to go on holiday together. An annual holiday, whether it's a week in a caravan or a month in a French gîte, is a wonderful way to set up a family tradition, plus it gives you a chance to bond with the grandchildren, and offers the parents a bit of respite and babysitting so they can have an evening or two out together.

Don't expect every moment to be joyous – the chances are, there'll be moments of tension, a few dark mutterings about 'Who left these muddy wellies here?' a few 'I did ask you not to give her chips so close to teatime' complaints – but it's a small price to pay for some solid time with your grandchildren, setting up happy memories of games, exploring, rockpool-fishing, long walks and picnics, or of boutique shopping, macaroon-eating, and restaurant meals, depending on what kind of holiday grandmother you are.

IF YOUR FAMILY LIVES ABROAD (OR YOU DO)

Everywhere's abroad to someone and out of sight doesn't have to mean out of mind. The world is smaller than it's ever been, with cheap flights to most European destinations, and all the technology that allows us to talk, even when we're miles apart. However, if they live in Ecuador and you live in England – or vice versa – it's not easy. Use Skype whenever you can, and save for a visit. If ill health or money trouble makes visiting impossible (or they're in the witness protection programme – unlikely, but hey, you never know) it may be a real source of sadness, but you can still write letters, make calls and share photos in various ways (see Chapter 8). This is where technology really comes into its own – and remember, nothing stays the same for ever, and just as you're getting used to being apart, you may get a call out of the blue . . .

IF YOU FALL OUT

The saddest reason to be apart is if you and your adult child (or their partner) have fallen out, and one or both sides refuses to kiss and make up. Family feuds are incredibly common; in fact, plenty of great literature revolves around contested wills, furious families, and enormous parental rifts. We've all said things we regret, or been unfairly accused of something we're sure we haven't done. And we've all felt righteous rage over someone else's bad behaviour.

But here's some advice: if it's remotely within your power to change the situation and open up lines of communication with your family – and particularly towards your grandchildren – then do it. It doesn't matter how much pride you have to swallow, or what was said and shouted three weeks or thirty years ago, it's never too late to try and build bridges. So be the bigger person, and do it.

Nobody ever got to the pearly gates to be greeted by St Peter smiling and saying, 'Well done for being so pig-headed all your life, and refusing to have any relationship with your family. You did well.' So sort it out. And if it's them who refuse to back down? It may be time to seek mediation, if only for the sake of the children who deserve as many loving adults in their lives as possible, and will never say, 'I'm glad Granny refused to speak to Dad throughout our entire childhood. It was for the best.' Because unless you're serving time for triple homicide, it probably isn't. Do everything in your power to kiss and make up.

CHAPTER 11

THE TROUBLE-SHOOTING GRAN

⟋ You forget how many ways small children have of not liking something, or for being upset. I had to dig into all my reserves of tact and patience. ⟍

Lynnette Wills, 55

By the time your grandchild is one or two, their personality will clearly be taking shape. And while obviously, that's almost certain to be delightful, unique, and genius-level, it doesn't mean that they'll always be easy to look after. Because once they learn that there are a whole raft of ways to express displeasure, like tiny medieval kings, they will exploit all of them. And if you happen to be looking after them at that point, it helps if you have a few coping mechanisms that go beyond 'Oh no, darling, don't do that.'

By the age of two, they will almost certainly have learned to say 'no' – and what a thrill that is. No to putting their coat on, no to eating their breakfast, no to going to sleep. The dilemma you have is how to turn it into a 'yes' without either being utterly feeble or breaking their spirit. As a gran, you're aiming for firm, kind and consistent. Of course, their parents might be those things too but most parents, subject to months of no sleep/thrown food/ endless screaming, will eventually break, and either burst into tears, shout back, or just phone you up and beg you to come over. So think of yourself as the Tantrum Cavalry, riding in when the infantry has been laid waste. And at that point, you're going to need a plan.

COMMON PROBLEMS AND HOW TO TACKLE THEM

Tantrums

Imagine being desperate to let the world know something crucially important, and yet every time you try to speak, all that comes out is a jumble of sounds. Now add in the notion that the thing you want most in the world has inexplicably been taken away, and someone is laughing off your pain and trying to shove you into a pushchair you don't want to be in, simultaneously. Frankly, who wouldn't have a tantrum?

It's no coincidence that the tantrum years ease off as the ability to communicate dramatically improves. So when a tantrum threatens, start from the point of view of your grandchild, and ask yourself, what is it they want that they can't have? Can they have it, in fact? If it's a stuffed toy that's been inadvertently placed out of reach, probably. If it's to sit on your knee and turn the steering wheel as you head down the motorway at 70 mph, probably not. So here's what to do:

AVERT IT

If at all possible, don't let it get to the tantrum stage. If they're not getting the attention they crave (because all toddlers are basically Broadway divas giving their final performance), stop what you're doing and give it to them. A two-year-old saying, 'Granny. Granny. Granny. GRANNY!' is not going to stop just because you're busy. She'll just get louder and louder until she explodes with grief and perceived neglect. So ask her what she wants, explain why she can't have it, and distract her with something else, fast.

Reward the good behaviour, ignore the bad, is the usual maxim, so if she's been quiet, tell her how good she is before she decides that quietness doesn't pay.

CONTROL IT

If it's too late, and she's already lying prone, screaming herself blue, the best thing you can do is make her feel safe. The more she screams, the more she frightens herself, so take firm hold of her, keep calm, and say soothing things until she stops bellowing and shuddering, at which point, mop her up and carry on with what you were doing. If she's lashing out and kicking, sit a little way away, but keep up the soothing chatter. It's hard not to panic, or yell back but don't. And if you're in a shop, do everything possible to carry her out of there and let her blow her gasket in the safety of the car/pushchair/park.

IGNORE IT

The best thing you can do is ignore it and carry on with what you were doing. That way they won't learn that they have the power to stop traffic and terrify adults – they will learn that tantrums don't work. Telling them off will only serve to frighten and upset them and if any telling-offs going to happen at this age, it's better coming from their mum or dad.

Lydia used to have terrible tantrums. I'd try and distract her with toys, biscuits, anything to hand, but if she wanted something she couldn't have, she would simply scream, throw herself to the floor and sob. I gradually realized that if I just sat nearby and said things like, 'Oh dear, what a shame,' and, 'You'll feel OK in a minute,' she would calm down, and when she came for a cuddle, we'd carry on as though nothing had happened. By the time she was four and talking properly, she'd grown out of them.

Sally Harris, 57

HATING SCHOOL

Some kids just don't like nursery. They'd rather be at home, with their mum, dad, or you, anything but to be stuck in playgroup or daycare with a load of scary kids. This often happens with only children, who are used to adult company. The whole concept of joining in with other tiny people who want to play with their toys is deeply upsetting and you're tasked with getting them through the door.

Their reluctance doesn't necessarily mean there's anything wrong, unless there's been a definite change of mood and behaviour since they started at nursery. A lot of this is simply down to personality, how robust they are, and whether they're an extrovert or prefer quiet reading to yelling hordes. If they're the latter, here's what to do:

* Comfort object: make sure he has his usual blanket, teddy or hoover bag with a face drawn on it – whatever floats his comfort boat.

* Try listing things that might be scaring him or draw pictures that he can point to. Some kids are scared of dogs, some of clowns, some of bouncy balls so trying to identify whether there's a significant person or thing he's frightened of is useful.

* It could simply be separation anxiety. Clinging to him, tears hovering in your eyes, murmuring 'Granny will be back soon! Granny will think of you ALL DAY!' (choking back sobs) is not the way to go. Firm, bright, brisk and positive is far more reassuring because you don't want your grandchild becoming convinced that his absence is so devastating to you that he can't possibly go inside. Go in fast, kiss goodbye, cheery wave, out. Much as if Special Forces did daycare.

✳   Ask him to complete a task during his day at nursery. Find out from the teacher or childminder what they're doing that day and say, 'I want to see the picture you draw of me,' then he'll spend the time before thinking about it, and the time after looking forward to telling you all about it.

DIFFERENT RULES AT HOME

If a small child is whining and complaining about something that seems perfectly reasonable to you – toast cut into triangles, not squares, or a cartoon being missed in favour of a visit to the park – the temptation is to tell them they're being a bit silly, and carry on with your toast/outing plans. But often, their distress is because small children are so wedded to routine that they can't bear any deviation from what they've come to expect. To you, it's a toast shape, to them it means the world has been thrown into chaos, and nothing is certain any more. So if you do things differently from how they do things at home, try bringing a familiar object from their house, such as a toy or even a bib or a cushion, to suggest continuity. It seems silly, but that might be all it takes to reassure her.

If you want them to sleep in a cot at home and a bed at your house, say, start by piling pillows around the bed, or pushing a playpen up against it, to give them the sense of security they're missing. Equally, with food, present it on a similar plate to the one they're used to, or give them the same drink to go with it.

SLEEP TROUBLE

Overtiredness and toddlers go together like early mornings and plastic trumpets. Inevitable but unpleasant. So assume that at some point, your grandchild will become immediately devastated over some small slight or thwarted hope, and will switch from sunny charmer to demonic, shrieking entity – probably in the middle of the busy supermarket. In which case, she is almost certainly exhausted, but too beside herself to go to sleep. At which point . . .

❊ There's no point trying to force her to go to sleep. Any rocking or soothing will probably be met with further screaming – so simply accept she's going to scream for a bit, and get her out of any major public areas.

❊ Put her in the car seat, and drive round and round in circles, on a pointless ride to nowhere, with the heating up reasonably high – nothing gets a child to sleep faster than consistent, boring movement. You can also try a bit of Mozart, which has been shown to act as a calming influence on babies' brain waves. Just make sure you don't fall asleep at the wheel.

❊ Never mind what the child care gurus say, this is a time, if ever there was one, for sticking her in front of a very soothing DVD.

SPOILT BEHAVIOUR

Few grannies have never worried that their grandchild is spoilt. Not in a Victorian, 'spare the rod and spoil the child' way (we hope) but in a 'too many toys, won't learn the value of anything, allowed to get away with murder' way. And often, it's true. Modern life conspires to create spoilt children, who may be showered with gifts every birthday and Christmas, allowed to stay up late on demand, given Lucky Charms for breakfast because they threaten tears, and permitted undreamed-of privileges when they're upset because working, busy or divorced (or all three) parents tend to live in a constant state of guilt and appeasement. This is not necessarily the fault of the parents – inconsistent rules at different homes, or fear of damaging children by being too harsh all play a part, and most parents are just doing their best. But if your grandchild is exhibiting a rather spoilt nature: whining, crying, ingratitude, throwing and generally behaving like a mad dictator in the last days of empire, try the following:

✳ Saying 'no'. It sounds easy, but under a barrage of demanding whinging, it's not. Far simpler to give in, get lunch made, and let them have what they want. But you're setting up a grim precedent if you do this, and they'll end up like those *X Factor* contestants who say to the judges, 'You're wrong, I'll be back!' even though they sing like a rusty tractor engine. Say no, and mean it. A spoilt child needs at least one consistent figure in his life.

✳ Criticize the behaviour, not the child. Say, 'It's much nicer when you say please and thank you,' not 'You're such a rude child.' Labelling small children with negatives isn't helpful, giving them firm guidance on the kind of behaviour you expect, is.

✳ Don't feel obliged to shower them with gifts, or give in when you're out shopping, when they threaten a tantrum if they can't have a toy. They're only little, and they're going to try everything in their arsenal to get what they want. Your job is to resist, unless you very much want them to have it. Good behaviour, however, should be rewarded. Bad should not.

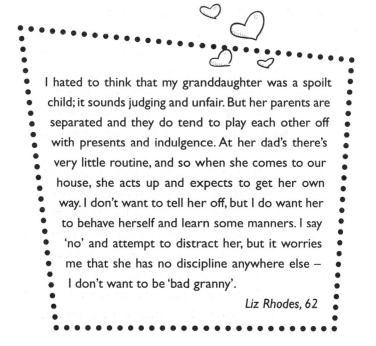

I hated to think that my granddaughter was a spoilt child; it sounds judging and unfair. But her parents are separated and they do tend to play each other off with presents and indulgence. At her dad's there's very little routine, and so when she comes to our house, she acts up and expects to get her own way. I don't want to tell her off, but I do want her to behave herself and learn some manners. I say 'no' and attempt to distract her, but it worries me that she has no discipline anywhere else – I don't want to be 'bad granny'.

Liz Rhodes, 62

NOT SHARING

If you have more than one grandchild, whether cousins or siblings, they will almost certainly fall out with each other at some point. The smaller they are, the more this is likely to happen, as the elder battles to exert their will, and the younger fights the power with all they've got (wiles, cunning and trickery, as opposed to brute force). This can also be an issue at the childminder's or nursery, so if sharing doesn't come naturally to your grandchild, but you don't want them to be hated for their grasping meanness, here's what to do:

❋ Remember that children under three don't really grasp the concept of sharing. They've seen a shiny tricycle, they want to ride it, it's not their problem if some other kid is standing in their way being difficult. So trying to explain the concept of 'mi casa es su casa' to a one-year-old is a complete waste of breath. Either find something else for the other child to play with or expect tears.

❋ As they get a little older, you can demonstrate the concept of sharing with food, but you can show them that you're cutting a sandwich in half and give them their halves on separate plates, to try and get across the concept of 'exactly the same each'.

❋ With toys and games, if sharing is proving problematic, you can employ an alarm clock. Explain that when the bell rings, it's time for the other one to have a go. You might still get tears, but little children do grasp the idea of fairness and unfairness, so explain they're getting precisely the same length of time with the toy, and you will make sure it is very fair indeed. They may not trust each other to do the right thing, but they will trust you.

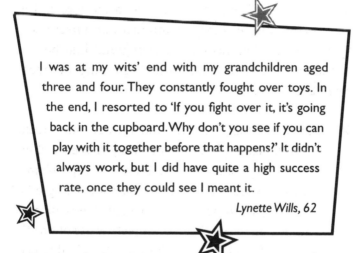

I was at my wits' end with my grandchildren aged three and four. They constantly fought over toys. In the end, I resorted to 'If you fight over it, it's going back in the cupboard. Why don't you see if you can play with it together before that happens?' It didn't always work, but I did have quite a high success rate, once they could see I meant it.

Lynette Wills, 62

EATING TROUBLE

Not the kind of eating trouble that requires specialist attention, or hospitalization and drips. Not even the kind where a baby spits out puree in an arc of contempt across the kitchen. More the kind where a toddler decides to be very picky indeed, and turn mealtimes into a battle of wills. Of course, some small children don't have a huge appetite. As long as they will eat certain foods, are gradually putting on weight, and don't seem hungry, tired or distressed, they're probably fine. But if your grandchild is developing a huge raft of foods they won't eat, or even consider, and they're not allergic, here are a few things to try:

◆ **PSYCHOLOGICAL CUNNING:** Serve yourself the food you'd like them to eat, without giving them any of it. Express delight, and add 'But I think you might be a bit little for this.' There's a good chance they will decide they are *not* too little, and insist on trying it themselves, as you continue to express doubt and amazement that they like this very grown-up substance.

◆ **FUN PRESENTATION:** This can be a bit of a bind if you end up with a child who won't eat anything that isn't arranged into a *trompe-l'oeil* Japanese garden, but making funny faces out of fruit slices, or hedgehogs out of mashed potatoes and sausages, can be a winner. Anything with a face is good as you can add 'Hedgehog will be sad if you don't eat all his spikes,' (and let's not go into the disturbing implications of this – they're only two).

◆ **ACCEPTANCE.** Do not turn meals into a battlefield. (If anyone's going to, it's their parents, not you.) Just remove the food without comment, and try again (with a fresh version, obviously, we're not Victorian governesses) later, when they really are hungry.

SULKING

There are few things as irritating as a wilfully sulky child. It's usually employed by children who lack the language skills to tell you how they feel, when they are hurt, angry or frustrated, but perhaps not confident or raging enough to throw a full tantrum. A sulk, however, can last for hours, resist all your jollying-along efforts, and make you feel as if you're battling a Scottish mist that's rolling through the house, bringing dampness and gloom in its wake. So here's what to do:

- **IGNORE IT:** It's hard to maintain a sulk when you're three and nobody is paying any attention to it. The chief reward of sulking is adults flocking round, worried and keen to cheer you up. A small child gains a lot of power this way though, of course, has no idea what to do with it. So pretend it's not happening and the lack of reward may snap them out of it.

- **UNCOVER THE PROBLEM:** It's easy to focus on the effect rather than the cause; a sulk can make you desperate to cure it. But trying to uncover what's beneath it may be more use. Is it a forbidden toy, a perceived unfairness, or a powerful desire for some particular food, trip or object? If so, negotiation or explanation may be possible but not unless you find out.

● **DISTRACTION:** The old classic but it works. Use the element of surprise convincingly – muttering 'Oh look, squirrel,' won't work, but crying 'Goodness! What's THAT?' might. Always take small toys when you go on outings and remember that low blood sugar can cause terrible glooms and sulks, so take some little snacks and a drink, too. Prevention is way better than cure.

SIBLING RIVALRY

This is very normal, Darwinian behaviour. A small child who's suddenly forced to welcome a new baby into his home is likely to behave like a king who has suddenly received news that a rival royal is raising an army and marching on his lands. Because as far as he's concerned, that's exactly what's happening. Sibling rivalry can last for years or even a lifetime. But the constant quarrelling and snatching is exhausting when you're tasked with looking after them both. So try:

✳ Not making them share. It sounds wildly counter-intuitive but it's important for little children to have their own things, which first and foremost are their own. If the toys at your house belong to everybody, it's confusing and annoying for them. If they have an equal amount of personal toys, plus a couple of joint ones (such as a dolls house or goal net) it's easier to convince them that sharing is OK.

✻ Don't always make them take turns – if one likes going swimming and the other likes crayoning, there's always going to be one who's reluctant when you do either. Instead, choose an activity they're both reasonably fond of, such as baking or feeding the ducks.

✻ Don't reward attention-seeking. If it's the little one's birthday and the older one is throwing herself about shrieking, it's because she's desperate to be back in the spotlight. Be calm, and tell her that her turn will come, and if that doesn't work, take her to a quiet place so she can burn out her rage without ruining her sibling's day. On no account buy her presents 'to stop her feeling jealous'. She needs to learn that sometimes, someone else gets a turn.

CLINGINESS

'Clingy' is a slightly old-fashioned word for 'insecure' or 'scared'. It's also extremely normal, and most children – all, in fact, but the boldest – go through periods of clinginess, often around times of change, such as a new baby arriving, or starting nursery. It can, however, be down to a tiny thing – something that frightened them in a TV programme, a dog that barked at them – anything that makes their world feel less secure. And if they're clinging to you, that's a sign they trust you 100 per cent. So here's how to handle it:

✳ Let her cling. No 18-year-old arrives at university, shrinking back and clutching his gran's hand. So they grow out of clinginess, and allowing them the reassurance they need as a toddler can help to convince them that the world is OK. Constantly detaching their hand, or getting cross, however, will reinforce their fears. Having said that, there are limits, and if you're barely allowed to nip to the loo, try the explaining method, where you break down their fears for them, and explain what will happen, and why: 'There are no big dogs in our house, because we haven't got room for any. So no big dogs can come in here. I'm going upstairs and I'll be back when I've been to the loo, so you don't need to be scared.' It's time-consuming but if they're old enough to grasp the basic point, it will work.

✳ Combine reassurance with jollity. He needs to know that you're not scared even if he is, so if you're dropping him off at nursery tell him, 'I'm coming to collect you after you've done some playing and had a nice time, then we'll go to the park', smile, kiss and wave. Hanging about, waving violently as if he's on the last transport to Iwo Jima, or hovering at the door of his classroom blowing kisses won't help – security and certainty will.

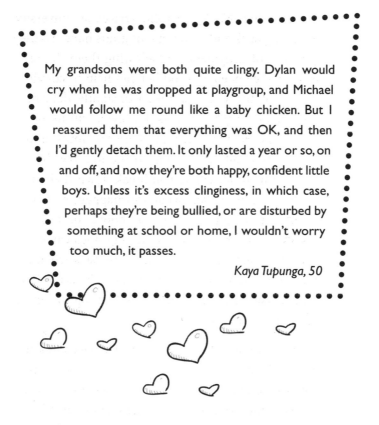

My grandsons were both quite clingy. Dylan would cry when he was dropped at playgroup, and Michael would follow me round like a baby chicken. But I reassured them that everything was OK, and then I'd gently detach them. It only lasted a year or so, on and off, and now they're both happy, confident little boys. Unless it's excess clinginess, in which case, perhaps they're being bullied, or are disturbed by something at school or home, I wouldn't worry too much, it passes.

Kaya Tupunga, 50

CHAPTER 12

WHAT KIND OF GRAN DO YOU WANT TO BE?

❝ It took me a little while to work out what kind of grandma I wanted to be – indulgent or firm but fair, cool or the voice of reason – you need to understand the kind of relationship you have with your new grandchild before it's clear. ❞

Alice Streeter, 61

So, you've met your new grandchild, or will do imminently. He or she is as adorable as you hoped, and now you've got years ahead in which to build your unique, gran-tastic relationship. You know how much time you can devote to your grandparenting, and how often you're likely to see them. But you may still be wondering exactly what kind of a grandma you're going to be. Because as we established to begin with, today's gran is rarely a comfy old body in a rocking chair. There are many possibilities: long-distance gran, single gran, full-on gran, part-time gran, step-gran, multi-gran with lots of grandkids, mum-and-gran when you've still got one child at home and another having babies, childcare gran, working gran, semi-retired gran . . . but whatever sort you are, by knowing your strengths and weaknesses, you can ensure you're the very best one possible.

If you're still not sure where your strengths lie, it's time to sum up – so take this quiz to see what kind of gran you really are . . .

WHAT KIND OF GRAN ARE YOU?

1 **The baby's just come home from hospital, and you're visiting. Are you:**

a. Warming a bottle with one hand while rocking her to sleep with the other arm

b. Reading the booklet the hospital gave your daughter, looking for instructions

c. Cooing at her, and re-winding the crib mobile every time it stops

d. Cracking open the champagne and exchanging 'terrifying birth' stories

e. Checking her over just in case the doctors missed anything

f. Unwrapping the gift you've bought and holding it up to her

2 She's about to put a button in her mouth. Do you:

a. Take it from her, and put it in the drawer marked 'things not safe for baby'

b. Take it from her and explain why she shouldn't put it in her mouth through the medium of mime

c. Take it off her and replace it with a chocolate button to distract her

d. Sigh and silently remove it, before going back to what you were doing

e. Drop and roll, snatch away the button, and call 999 to be sure you did the right thing

f. Take it from her and put it in the button box you're collecting for when she's older and can play with them

3 You're at the park, and a bigger child pushes your grandson. Do you:

a. Dust him down, check he's OK, tell the bigger child off, and seek out his parent to have a word

b. Take the bigger child aside and explain why it's not OK to push people

c. Rush your grandson to the car and cuddle him better

d. Brush him down, say 'no harm done', and keep an eye on the big lad

e. Check him all over for abrasions, bruising or lesions, and apply a plaster to the spot where he was pushed

f. Determine that it won't spoil your park visit and head off to the duck pond instead

4 **You're eating dinner and your one-year-old grand-daughter is itching to try it. Do you:**

a. Give her her own portion, served on a tiny plate

b. Explain why it's too grown up for her. You've never to little to understand nutrition

c. Let her scoop a bit up with her fingers

d. Offer her a tiny bit on your fork

e. Google 'beef stew' to see if there's anything in it that she really shouldn't eat

f. Decide she won't like it, but she might like the puréed version you made just in case

5 **You're taking your grandchild for a day out. Where are you going?**

a. The park, the shops, the soft play area, the children's cafe and the playground

b. The museum, or the art gallery

c. The Disney Store, the zoo, or the aquarium

d. You'll probably nip to the shops, then perhaps the baby playground

e. Anywhere you can carry out a full risk-assessment before you go

f. Nowhere, she likes being at your house best

MOSTLY A: **FULL-ON GRAN**

Are you exhausted? Even if the baby's not yet born, you're probably worn out from knitting blankets, making mobiles and reading up on nutrition. There is no area of gran-dom in which you don't excel, and you're determined to cover all bases. Your grandchild wants to climb Everest? Fine, then you'll find out how that's possible, and action the fundraising. Your grandchild wants to bake halloween cookies in the shape of a haunted house with smoke coming out of the chimney? Then that's going to happen even if you have to design a cookie template yourself. You're there with the camera at every school play, cheering from the sideline at every football match, and happy to cook meals, change sicked-on bedding and support their entire life journey, from midnight feeds to university applications.

And that's great but while gran burn-out isn't a recognized medical condition, it is possible. And if it's all down to your determination to be a better gran than you were a mum, perhaps because you were a single parent and pressed for time, or you worked away a lot and feel guilty, the fact is, you need to try and let that go. Because it's not about your grandchild's needs, it's about your own. Grandchildren do just fine knowing that their gran loves them and will be around when they need her. You don't need to treat your relationship like an ongoing audition. Cut yourself some slack, and let the parents take the strain sometimes. After all, you've already done the parenting and being able to step back occasionally is the whole point of being a grandma.

MOSTLY B: **EDUCATIONAL GRAN**

You're determined to improve your grandchild's chances in life because you're convinced that knowledge is power, and the more you explain, the happier your grandchildren will be. You won't let a single opportunity to impart knowledge pass you by, whether that's explaining why they shouldn't eat cat litter (even when they're six months old) or talking them through the finer points of the Napoleonic Wars when you happen to pass a statue of the man on horseback. It's possible that you are already a teacher, and it just happens to come naturally, but even if you're not, you're convinced that they must be taught how the world works, from the moment they emerge into it. You never stop educating yourself either, your bookshelves probably groan with child-care manuals, and your web browser is stuffed with baby advice sites and early years education apps.

This is all admirable – who doesn't want to give their small loved ones the best chance to shine? But it's also easy to forget that what's endlessly fascinating to you might possibly be a little bit dull to the average four-year-old, and that it's useful to tailor your knowledge to their powers of absorption. Otherwise their entire childhood can begin to feel like an exam and one which they might be failing.

By all means tell them things but try to intersperse your educational outings and books with some genuine rolling-on-the-floor fun as well. Cuddles, television, cakes and silly games may not feel educational but they will do wonders for self-esteem and lifelong memories – both yours and theirs.

MOSTLY C: **INDULGENT GRAN**

You dedicate most of your waking hours to your grandchild's happiness. If you're not already a full-time carer to her, you almost certainly spend the vast majority of your time thinking about her and devising ways to make her life happier.

Nothing is too much trouble: if she wants to throw you out of bed and sleep there herself dressed as Princess Elsa, you'll let her, and if she cries, you'll run through every possible solution before you're prepared to give up and just let her cry.

This, of course, makes you a deeply loving gran, but it also means you might be making a rod for your own back. When you're this dedicated to someone's needs, it can be difficult to inject any discipline, and as she grows up, she's going to need boundaries. Ones that you may need to set. So if you indulge her every whim, and anticipate her every desire, it could be a long road. Keep your loving nature, and the special treats you want to share with her but remember that setting boundaries is an act of kindness to small children, otherwise they don't know what's OK and it's confusing for them once they're back home. A happy balance of indulgence and management is ideal.

MOSTLY D: **COOL GRAN**

You're so laid back, on your watch your grandchildren should be wearing shades and lying in hammocks. Unlike many new grans, you're not remotely fazed by your new role; in fact, you've taken to it entirely naturally. You see grandmotherhood as just one more in your portfolio of life roles: mother, partner, businesswoman, mistress (well, maybe not but then again . . .)

You're at ease with child care, but you're not about to let your grandchild dictate the pace – if you're planning to go to the shops that's exactly what you'll do, regardless of whether or not they're throwing a tantrum, or whining to stay to home. It's your view that children fit into adults' lives, and not the other way around, while at the same time, you're willing to meet them halfway, with a little indulgence from time to time.

And that's great, your grandchildren will grow up aware that the world does not revolve around their tiny, powdered bottoms, and you'll get a balance of full-on gran time and space to think. The only danger is that you'll be so laid back, you may not always notice immediately when you should be intervening.

Your determination to take everything in your stride may also mean you're a little laissez-faire when it comes to sharp corners, easily swallowed nuts, and inappropriate TV programmes. It's highly unlikely your grandchildren will come to any harm with you in charge but it pays to remember that you're not their mum and that you are answerable to their real parents. They'll be at ease in your company and when they're teenagers, you'll be the one persuading their parents to let them get their ears pierced.

MOSTLY E: **ANXIOUS GRAN**

You are a one-woman SWAT team. Your grandchild is going nowhere that you haven't already scanned for danger. The idea that any harm could befall him while in your care is terrifying to you and you're not about to take that risk. If you could, you'd pad your entire house with cushions, cook only with knitted pans and tepid water, and permit no toys with hard edges, in case he inadvertently falls forward onto them and hurts himself. It's good for the parents to know that you're so careful, and so well versed in first-aid. But it's a burden of worry you carry everywhere with you, that could be avoided.

No one wants to put their precious grandchild in a position where he could come to serious harm but a few bumps and scratches are part of growing up and learning to take care of himself. So while in babyhood, your refusal to let him push the edges of his capabilities might be OK, by the time he's four or five, you could be dealing with some serious tantrums and frustrations if you refuse to ever let him swing in the park, climb on a wall, or play with bigger kids and risk getting a shove or two.

Your worry comes from a kind and caring place but it also suggests a lack of trust in yourself. Perhaps it's a long time since you raised your own children, or perhaps one of them had an accident that you've always blamed yourself for. The truth is, you're perfectly capable of looking after a baby without wrapping him in fifteen layers of cotton wool. So try to trust yourself more, and more importantly as they grow up, trust them to recover from a slight bump. Children are a lot more resilient than you think.

MOSTLY F: **SPECIAL TREAT GRAN**

It's likely you don't see your grandchild all the time, so when you do it's a pretty big treat, for both of you. You enjoy thinking of ways to maximize your time together, and hope that they'll come to see visits to your house as a very enjoyable break from the norm. And in many ways, that's the best kind of gran to be – where you drop into their lives, magically improve everything, and then leave them for a bit to get on with their normal life. Of course, it may be a source of sadness that you can't see more of them but it's true in your case that absence makes the heart grow fonder and that a little of what you fancy does you good.

You're a big believer in that, and while you're not about to flout any major parental rules, you can't help thinking that an occasional extra treat, whether it's staying up late or a little present when it's not a special occasion, won't do any harm.

Because you're not with her all the time, you can think ahead to the future as well, perhaps saving up for her college years, or planning holidays and trips that you can take together when she's old enough. It's lovely for your grandchildren to have time with you to look forward to, but don't forget you can also have plenty of contact in the here and now, thanks to technology, and whereas once, you might have been reduced to yearly visits, now you can Skype a couple of times a month, Facebook weekly, or chat on Facetime as soon as she's old enough to look at the camera.

And though you'll miss her, don't forget that it's lovely to be the person who brings magic with them when they visit and is missed when they leave. Being a grandmother means you have a unique relationship, no matter how often you see your grandchildren.

Perhaps you already know exactly what sort of gran you are, or you're still working it out. Maybe things are exactly the way you want them, with your loved ones around the corner and plenty of time to see them. Or perhaps you're worried about ill health, or your son getting a job in Australia, or the baby's persistent cough. Nobody ever said being a gran, and having so much love for a whole new person, was easy. You thought you'd got your worrying out of the way with your own kids, and it turns out you've now got a whole new set of things to fret about. But you've also got a whole new role to embrace.

And while being a parent is full-on, the joy of being a granny is that you can give all the love you've got and still hand them back after the allotted time. You're also more likely to be patient, you'll have more time to devote to their needs and conversation, and you won't be worrying about setting the rules, because the parents have already done that.

Being a grandma isn't always wonderful, of course. But as family relationships go, it really is one of the very best roles you can have, so make the most of it. Because one day, you might be a great-granny and you need to start getting the practice in now.

Acknowledgements

Thanks to all the grandmas, grans, grannies and nannas who told their stories in this book; and thanks too to Janey, Pete, Joan, David, Vera and Les for being the best grandparents anyone could ask for.

Index